TRIUMPH TR2/3/3A

Bill Piggott

CONTENTS

Foulis

Haynes

A FOULIS Motoring Book

First published 1987

© **Haynes Publishing Group**

Published by:
Haynes Publishing Group,
Sparkford, Near Yeovil,
Somerset BA22 7JJ

Haynes Publications Inc.
861 Lawrence Drive, Newbury
Park, California 91320, USA

**British Library Cataloguing in
Publication Data**

Piggott, Bill
Triumph TR2/3/3A super profile.
—(Super Profile)
1. Triumph automobile—History
I. Title   II. Series
629.2'222   TL215.T7

ISBN 0-85429-559-3

Library of Congress Catalog Card No.
86-82630

Editor: Robert Iles

Series photographer: Andrew
Morland
Road tests: Courtesy of *Motor
Sport, The Motor, Autosport*
Page layout: Dave Self
Printed in England, by:
J.H. Haynes & Co. Ltd

Further titles in this series will be published at regular intervals. For information on new titles please contact your bookseller or write to the publisher.

FOREWORD

I can still recall the first time I became aware of the TR2: at the impressionable age of 7, I was taken by my father to the Goodwood 9 hour race one hot August afternoon in 1955. In the car park we parked adjacent to a gleaming British Racing Green TR2, sporting wire wheels with enamel 'Union Jack' badges on its scuttle. The simple, clean but rugged lines of the bodywork, and the rakish cutaway doors gave an impression of speed and fitness for purpose that left its mark, and I resolved one day to own such a car. The faster, noisier, more expensive machines on the track for some reason touched me less — maybe even at that age I was sufficient of a realist to see that the TR was a practical, economical and above all usable car that one really could eventually possess, whereas "D type" Jaguars and Ferraris were for heroes! When later I heard that TR2 exhaust note, the splendid "TR roar", and was given a Dinky Toy model of the car, which I have to this day, I became completely subjugated.

The first TR was shown to the World initially at the 1952 London Show, but that vehicle was a long way from the item that later enthralled me at Goodwood. The reception accorded to the "Triumph Sports" as it was then called was moderate indeed. However, before two years had passed, many minds had been changed, and many words had been eaten. The TR2 showed itself to be the perfect compromise sports car — suitable for shopping, commuting and going on holiday on the one hand, yet excellent at dicing and competition with very little modification on the other — it was fast, robust, economical, reliable and above all cheap.

Fortunately for us today, the inbuilt strength of the TR has ensured that a good many survive all over the World. This high survival rate coupled with the large number manufactured ensured that for some years TRs were undervalued relative to other classic two seaters, sheer numbers available helping to keep prices low to a point where it wasn't worth renovating or even properly maintaining them. Happily, those days are over, and the TR is appreciated for its own qualities. For more than 15 years now I have owned and driven TRs since the days when they cost more to insure than to buy!

I have made lasting friendships through this interest, principally through the world wide network of contacts provided by the TR Register. Without the help of this Club, I could not have written this book.

My thanks must also go to Austin Rover PLC for the use of items from their photographic archives, the National Motor Museum at Beaulieu, the Editors of Motor Sport, Autocar, Motor and Autosport Magazines for permission to use Road Test material and photographs, and to Mr. Clausager of the British Motor Industry Heritage Trust. Thanks are due also to Brian Blackwell, and to Tony Price, Mel Francis and Geoffrey Goodall for providing their TRs for photography by Andrew Morland, to the Westbury Quarry, Westbury-sub-Mendip, Somerset for use of their premises as a photographic location. I must mention also the debt that all TR enthusiasts owe to Graham Robson, for his original and fascinating research into TR history. In addition, thanks go to various TR enthusiasts who have allowed me to use photographs from their collections, and to Neil Revington and Geoffrey Goodall for assistance with the "Owner's View" section. From the TR Register I must mention the assistance I have had from Val Simpson, Ginny Soden and Keith Wigglesworth, whose help has been invaluable.

My thanks are also due to my Secretary, Mrs. Cynthia Ellis for typing the manuscript, and finally for all her help and encouragement to my wife Claire, who travelled in TRs long before I did!

Bill Piggott.

HISTORY

The TR Series did not so much take the Motoring World by storm as clamber aboard by dint of arduous hours of development, and finally by results where and when they mattered, on road and track and in the market place.

At the commencement of the 1950's, available British sports cars were either of the square-rigged, somewhat pedestrian, MG style, or alternatively of the super-fast "dream machine" XK120 type. Nothing was available in-between to cover the $1^1/2$ to $2^1/2$ litre market, and it was apparent to many people that a definite niche for such a car existed, especially in the prosperous USA. Then, as now, export or die was the demand, and such sports cars as were being made were almost all sent abroad. Sir John Black of Standard-Triumph could see this gap in the market, and in addition, particularly wanted to produce a successful sports model to be the flag-ship for his Company. Nothing ambitious in the terms of numbers was contemplated, nor in his most optimistic mood could Sir John have envisaged the numbers of TRs that were eventually assembled. Other plans were being laid elsewhere, principally by Donald Healey to produce what became the (Austin) Healey 100, and by MG to update their experimental car into the MGA. The MGA launch was delayed

until 1955, but the Austin Healey appeared at the 1952 London Motor Show, at the same time as the new Triumph Sports was revealed; although the Triumph was seen very much as an "also ran" to the Healey at first, things certainly changed later!

Sir John Black's long-standing desire for a sports model had initially, but only partially, been satisfied by Triumph's Roadster model of 1946, originally an 1800cc car but later incorporating the 2 litre Vanguard engine destined to go ultimately into the TR series. This car, whilst successful in a limited way, was both expensive to make and relatively unsporting, being more of a coupe than a true sports car. It had not been in production long when Black asked Walter Belgrove, the Company's principal stylist, for a completely revised design, giving him a very free hand within limitations of the use of a Vanguard-type chassis and engine. With this brief, Belgrove produced the extraordinary TRX of 1950, an unusual and futuristic roadster with a hydraulically operated hood and headlamps, complex and expensive double-skinned bodywork, and styling described variously as cigar or bullet shaped. The car was somewhat "boulevard" in concept, and would probably have gone down tolerably well in parts of the USA; it was not however a sports car. The weight was considerable, the performance barely better than the superseded Roadster 2000, and the Press reception was poor. Following considerable vacillation within the Company, the project was firstly suspended, and finally by the end of 1951 virtually abandoned, with only three prototypes having been made. This left Black without even the semblance of a sporting car in his range, or even on the horizon. It was during this period that an abortive attempt was made to purchase the Morgan Car Company as a going concern,

Morgans already utilising the Company's Vanguard engine. Presumably the principle was if you can't beat them, buy them! Morgan resisted, and so finally in early 1952 Standard-Triumph had another attempt at a sports model.

There had been in existence for some time a privately built Special, known as "Buttercup", constructed by one Ken Rawlings from Standard components and including a Vanguard engine. Being of light weight, this little car had considerable performance and was really the TR2's ancestor, although it has always been said that neither Black nor Alick Dick his successor knew of it at the time. Be that as it may, the decision was taken to have a new Triumph Sports ready for the London Show in October 1952, costs to be kept to a minimum. Harry Webster, the Chief Designer, was instructed to use parts from sources within Standard-Triumph wherever possible, the use of the Vanguard engine being essential. Styling, to be kept as simple as possible to control tooling costs, was again by Walter Belgrove, and the whole project was scheduled for rapid completion. Body panel curvature was kept simple, panels were made bolt-on where possible, bonnet and boot hinges were external and existing proprietary units used where available. A chassis frame based on the pre-War Standard "Flying Nine" was employed, together with Triumph Mayflower front suspension and a Mayflower rear axle, which was to prove the car's Achilles Heel for some years. The Vanguard engine was initially modified to produce 75 bhp, capacity being reduced to 1991cc to creep into the under 2-litre class, so clearly competition activities were in the corporate mind. Twin SU carburettors were fitted, de rigeur for the sporting motor of the day; the gearbox was a four-speed version of the Vanguard item, only slightly modified. The two-seater body differed from the production TR in having a sloping tail with the externally mounted spare wheel fixed acrosswise, thirties style. There was no boot, just a space for luggage behind the seats.

This device was built in a very short time, and the aim was to sell it for a basic price of £500 plus tax, providing the customer with a 90 miles per hour top speed. The prototype just made the Earls Court Show, but in truth had hardly run, let alone been properly tested, so scepticism from those in the know was considerable. Compared with the much more developed Austin Healey 100, which had by then proved its capabilities in an Autosport Road Test published simultaneously with the Show's opening, the "Triumph Sports" as it was billed was a very unknown quantity. Incidentally, the epithet "TR1" was never used, and the prototype has only come to be called that in more recent times. The price was finally fixed at £555 plus tax, and whether 90 miles per hour was achievable was not certain. Reasonable interest was shown in the new car, and immediately after the Show certain motoring journalists were given the opportunity to try out the only existing vehicle. Evidently their reaction was not over-enthusiastic, although polite – in those days it must not be forgotten that road-testers were nothing like as candid as today, and the worst that a bad car could expect to receive was a veiled hint of "modified rapture". No road tests of the Triumph Sports were published, so we cannot now know more of this car, for it ceased to exist in original form shortly afterwards. Before that however, Sir John Black had taken the portentious decision to ask Ken Richardson to assess this TR. Richardson was a test driver and development engineer with the BRM concern, and also had a reputation as a talented racing man. Clearly his opinion, as the

first outside engineer to try the car, would be of value. History relates that his opinion of the vehicle was not high, Richardson evidently calling the car a "death trap" after just a short drive. Contrary to what one might have expected having regard to Black's forceful personality, Richardson was not reviled, but rather was asked to join the Company to assist with developing this "death trap " into a proper sports car. He agreed, and embarked with the rest of the design team on what amounted to a major redesign of the whole project, together with a most arduous series of running and proving trials, including many hours of driving at 100 miles per hour on the MIRA banked track. Popular opinion has held that Ken Richardson was personally solely responsible for the creation of the TR2 from the Triumph Sports. Whilst undoubtedly he played the major role and utilised his high-speed experience to good effect, there can be no doubt that during those months from November 1952 to the Spring of 1953 the whole team was involved, many problems being identified and successfully overcome.

Changes

The fundamental instability of the original car was quickly put down to the Flying Nine type chassis, which simply lacked the rigidity necessary to deal with the speeds and cornering forces now being asked of it. The redesign of this item was so total that the final article, although bearing a general resemblance to the original in layout and dimension, actually contained no common pressings, and was of course very much stronger. Engine development proceeded in stages, and eventually a combination of twin SU's, larger inlet valves, 8.5 to 1 compression ratio and a high lift

camshaft, combined with fine tuning and adjustment produced 90 bhp. To counteract this performance the front brakes were increased in diameter to ten inches. This power output was sufficient to give the TR a genuine 100 miles per hour top speed, together with an efficiency that led to extraordinary fuel economy, as road testers would later find out.

In February 1953, Black had taken the Triumph Sports to the U.S.A. for display, the car presumably in a halfway stage of development towards the TR2, although a contemporary photographs shows it still had its round tail. Subsequent body development included adding some inches to the rear, to provide a very practical (and large for a two-seater car) luggage boot, the spare wheel being placed horizontally beneath the boot in its own compartment, accessible from without by a trap door. A slight bow was introduced to the windscreen, but the doors, scuttle, front wings and front apron panel were left much as previously. The sum total of the changes amounted to a more purposeful and certainly more useful vehicle. By now known as the TR2, two prototypes existed, MVC575 and MWK950. Incredibly, both these cars survive in the hands of a British enthusiast, whose long term aim it is to restore them. Upon examination of MVC575, tangible evidence has come to light that this car incorporates at least some of the remains of the original 1952 Show car, which had previously been thought to have been scrapped.

Success

The whole Triumph Sports to TR2 transformation took barely five months, and the new TR2 was shown to the public at the Geneva Motor Show in March 1953. By this time, Black, Richardson & Co.

realised that the pile of hastily-cobbled pieces had been developed into a potential winner, both road and track worthy, capable of high speed and with excellent acceleration. Estimates of numbers to be produced were thus revised and tooling and materials were ordered. Having regard however to the lukewarm reception given to the original car barely six months before, a considerable "credibility gap" still existed, and it was to bridge this that Black authorised Richardson to try for 120 mph in May 1953 with one of the prototypes, MVC575. Ken Richardson knew his car was capable of around 110 in standard trim, and felt confident that with certain bodywork streamlining it would achieve the desired figure. Accordingly an aeroscreen, passenger-side metal cockpit cover, undershield and rear wheel spats were fitted, all items subsequently offered to the public. Overdrive was used, but the engine was reputedly in standard tune. The car was taken to the Ostend to Jabbeke highway in Belguim, and early on the morning of the 20th May was put to the test. As is now well known, it achieved only 104 mph on its first run, but as a plug lead had come loose, this was on three cylinders! Fully operational, the car managed more than 124 mph on a two way run, handsomely exceeding everyone's expectations and capturing headlines as desired. Even with full windscreen, hood and sidescreens fitted, 114 mph was achieved, although this was cheating somewhat in that the undershield was still in place. Editorials appeared in the motoring press, large advertisements were placed, and potential orders were arriving. Optimism rather than scepticism now prevailed, and it really began to look as though Standard-Triumph had the sports car it had so long sought.

The TR2 was at least as fast as the Austin Healey, considerably cheaper, much more economical and nor did it suffer the Healey's embarrassing ground clearance problems. As compared with the TD/TF MGs, it was no-contest, and it even looked as if the TR would be giving the XK120 a run for its money. The only problem was that the TR, for all its new-found virtues, simply was not available. Right into July 1953 only the prototypes existed, whereas the Austin Healey was actually on sale and being delivered to private owners by this time. The delay was caused, of course, by the redesign, and having regard to this, Standard-Triumph did very well to get production started in the late Summer of 1953, still barely a year from the hasty manufacture and showing of the original vehicle.

My own research into the early TR2 build records shows how production built up: TS1 and 2 were built by the 22nd July, but then some days elapsed until TS3 and 4 were made on the 12th August. Six more cars were constructed before the end of August, but by the finish of September, TS25 had been reached and cars were being made at the rate of one a day, 35 being made in October. The great majority of these vehicles were non-overdrive, basic specification left-hand-drive cars, and most were finished in either Ice Blue or Pearl White. Four or five cars were being made daily by the end of November, and on the last day of the year, the 300th production TR2 was built. Of these 300 1953 built cars, 209 were left-hand-drive, 44 were fitted with overdrive, 96 were finished in Pearl White, 94 in Ice Blue, 50 in Geranium, 44 in Black, and a mere 16 in Olive Yellow. The price had risen to £595 plus tax ex-works, but even so, this was about the cheapest way to enjoy 100 miles per hour motoring. Most cars were exported to North America, and of the right-hand-drive cars that stayed in the UK, believed to be around 50, many were supplied to Standard-Triumph dealerships spread evenly about the country so that maximum exposure could be guaranteed. Very few reached private individuals in the UK, and a waiting list was quickly established. However, some cars inevitably found their way into the hands of the rally drivers of the day, who rapidly realised that in the TR2 they had a potential outright winner. The 1953 racing season had of course been missed, so the car's UK competition debut was in the various rallying events during the 1953/4 Winter. The first action of some enthusiasts upon receiving their TR2s was to respray them, as Standard-Triumph had misinterpreted the market with their range of somewhat effeminate colours. Thus British Racing Green and Bright Red TR2s began appearing even prior to the factory revising the colours available in April 1954. It was difficult enough to get a new TR2, let alone worry about in which colour it was finished, and some amazing factory combinations were produced around this time, the nadir being surely the few cars produced in Olive Yellow with Geranium (pink) leather trim and Geranium hoods and sidescreens!

Deliveries began to improve in early 1954, which was just as well, for demand for the car increased dramatically consequent upon the results of the 1954 RAC Rally, held in those days in March. Not only did the TR2 win outright (J.C. Wallwork) and come second (P.G. Cooper), the car also took

the Ladies prize (Mary Walker) and came second in the team prize, not bad for a car hitherto largely unproven. Now the TR had to be taken seriously, and a string of rally successes matched by no other contemporary model ensued over the next six years. The TR2 and its successors became essential wear for rally exponents, and nor was the race track neglected. In June 1954 OKV 777 was the car selected to be entered for Le Mans, ostensibly as a private entry by Wadsworth and Dickson; there was some covert works support, and the car ran excellently, averaging nearly 75 mph for 24 hours and at 34 miles to the gallon! It finished 15th overall, a highly creditable result for it was almost wholly to standard specification, more so than probably any other car competing. Just prior to this Le Mans event, the Mille Miglia had taken place in Italy, and a single works entered TR2 (OVC 276) had taken 27th place, driven by Ken Richardson himself together with Rally Driver Maurice Gatsonides. This car was also relatively standard, although it did run on 16 inch wire wheels to raise the overall gearing. Once again, like the prototypes, it is surprising to find that both these hard-worked cars have survived and are today owned by TR Register members.

In the Alpine Rally that summer, three factory TR2s were entered, one winning a Coupe des Alpes for the versatile Gatsonides. Success followed success throughout 1954 and into 1955, both in amateur hands in Club events, and in the hands of the works team in full International events. Two teams each of three TR2s entered the RAC Tourist Trophy Race in Northern Ireland in September, and all six cars finished. Whilst outclassed by the Jaguars, the Triumphs won both first and second team prizes, again proving totally reliable.

Mention should perhaps be

made at this stage of the Swallow Doretti, which was an independently produced sports car based very largely on TR2 mechanical parts, but with a very attractive double-skinned aluminium body. This was the principal ''spin-off'' from TR production at this time, although Triumph's Belgian Importers produced a car called the TR2 Francorchamps, which was a TR2 with a fixed-head-coupe top and winding windows, together with other styling embellishments. By September, nearly 3,500 TR2s had been made, about two thirds of which had been exported. The model had become a major success, and a large money earner for Standard-Triumph. Sir John Black had his real sports car after years of trying, the only problem being that he had become ill following a motor accident just outside the works gates, which had led to his resignation early in 1954. Thus ironically, he was no longer in charge when the real breakthrough occurred. Ken Richardson however continued on the staff to run the works competition department, which he did with great success almost to the end of the TR3A's production run.

The road test reports on the TR2 had been favourable, except for frequent mention of the incredibly noisy exhaust system, and the car's noteworthy fuel economy. Many private owners who did not use all the performance found overall m.p.g. figures in the high 30s quite easy to obtain, even 40 miles per gallon being possible with care. It was a TR2 that won the well known Mobilgas Economy Run in 1955 with the truly amazing figure of 71 miles to the gallon. This same car, SYA 176 owned by Richard Benstead-Smith, also proved eminently versatile, winning the Vintage Sports Car Club's Pomeroy Trophy Competition in the same year.

At the 1954 London Show

basic price was increased again to £625, and several changes were incorporated, as detailed elsewhere in this book. Introduction of the sill below the doors was welcomed, and this modification has led to the earlier 1953/4 TR2s becoming known as ''Long Door'' models today. As quite a number of surviving cars built with long doors have had the sills and shorter doors fitted over the years, a genuine long-door TR2 is a rare vehicle today. In 1955, at Le Mans, a team of three works TR2s was entered, all having front disc brakes, one having rear disc brakes as well; they were more experimental than the 1954 car, and averaged around 84 miles per hour, all three finishing the race. TR competition success had by now become so frequent that it is impossible to go into detail in the space available. Suffice it to say that Richardson's works TR3s and 3As, the latter originally finished in the special colour of Apple Green, were always in contention for class wins, team prizes and sometimes outright wins in International events. In Club rally events no car had more success, and the TR had truly become ''Joe Public's off the shelf do-it-all Sports Car''.

What next?

The TR3 replaced the TR2 at the 1955 London Show, the price going up again to £650 basic, then rapidly to £680, for Standard-Triumph were able to capitalise on their success. The big news in late 1956 was the introduction of the Girling front disc brake system on the production TR3. Apart from a few sports-racing cars, this was the first application of disc brakes to a genuine production car, and very successful they were. The stopping power was improved, but it was their anti-fade qualities that really gave discs their superiority. Power output was by now up to 100 bhp, but the car had put on some weight compared to the earlier TRs and performance was thus no better. Fuel consumption suffered somewhat, and this pattern was repeated right through to the end of TR4A production in 1967, performance being still very similar to that of the original TR2! Creature comforts had improved considerably of course, but that's another story!

As can be seen from the list in the following chapter, a vast amount of optional equipment was available for the TR, possibly more than for any other car at the time. Some of the items were, and are, very rare, such as the rear wheel spats, and I have never met anyone who has seen a factory undershield! Other extras were somewhat esoteric, such as the "fitted" suitcase, shaped with a sloping top to match the interior profile of the boot! Wire wheels were not specified as original equipment on more than about 20% of cars, but many survivors have been retrospectively fitted with these, for the conversion is straightforward. Overdrive was specified on perhaps 25% to 30% of new TRs, and once again this has frequently been fitted subsequently. Anyone who has tried a TR with good three-speed overdrive unit would not be content to drive a non-overdrive TR thereafter.

In late 1957, a further revision of the TR took place, with the TR3A being introduced. Initially this was for the American market, the first few thousand cars produced being sent there. The front badge still read TR3, and the car was not called the TR3A by the works, at least not for some time. The principal revisions were new style seats, a full-width grille with more recessed headlights, new front bumper arrangements and external door and boot handles. Price had risen again to £699 basic, but even so sales of

the TR really began to take off during 1958, accelerating even further in 1959. Nearly 38,000 cars were produced in the two years from the introduction of the 3A model to the retooling of the bodywork in late 1959, an excellent figure for a pure sports model. This bodywork retooling took place after nearly 60,000 cars had been made, and was probably necessitated by the original tools becoming worn out. The opportunity was taken to alter certain minor features of the body pressings, although viewed externally the car was virtually identical.

Competition successes continued, with a Coupe des Alpes in 1958, outright victory to Paddy Hopkirk in the Circuit of Ireland event, Class wins in the Tulip Rally and success in the Monte Carlo and Liege-Rome-Liege events. At home, so many TRs were appearing on the race tracks that some meetings contained special races exclusively for the model! The TR was the ideal club sports car, cheap and easy to tune, safe, fast and above all reliable, which was comprehensively demonstrated in July 1959 when a team of Cambridge University Undergraduates broke eight International long distance records, covering 10,000 kilometres at 102 miles per hour. Also in 1959, Triumph decided after several years of absence to revisit Le Mans with a works team, this time on a more serious basis than previously. A twin-cam

engine was designed for the race, but always with the possibility of marketing it as a production option should it prove sucessful. The bodywork of these new cars was largely TR3A shaped, although a six inch longer wheelbase was incorporated. Three of these cars were built, but unfortunately none finished the race. In 1960 and 1961 further teams of twin-cam TRs were entered for Le Mans, but by now the body had grown more akin to the TR4. In 1960 all finished but failed to qualify on minimum distance regulations, but in 1961 all three such cars not only finished, but took the team prize.

TR3A production was in full swing throughout 1960, very few modifications being made to the design during the final years. However, a recession hit the Motor Industry towards the end of 1960, and for the first time TRs became difficult to sell, stocks beginning to accumulate. Even without this general recession, the fact that the basic design (however successful) had been in production for more than seven years was beginning to tell, and although the TR4 as a replacement for the TR3A was in the design stage, it was not ready for production. Standard-Triumph were themselves in financial trouble at this time, which culminated in the takeover of the Company by Leyland Vehicles; this led to considerable economies being made, one of which was the closure of the competitions department and the departure of Ken Richardson, who was not best pleased. Production of the 3A series finally ceased in September/October 1961, having slowed down considerably during that last year. The final car built was number TS82346; stocks in hand ensured that the model was still available new well into 1962, some UK cars not being first registered until the Summer, by which time the replacement TR4 was generally available.

Curiously there is a postscript to the TR story in that the demise of the 3A was not quite the end of the sidescreen TR production. A number of the "die-hard" brigade in North America did not care for the new TR4, with its softer image, winding windows and full height doors. They demanded, and more surprisingly got, a further run of early TRs, the TR3Bs. Sold only across the Atlantic, these cars were made during 1962 in two series; firstly the TSF series, being TR3As in all but name, and secondly the TCF series, incorporating as standard the 86mm bore 2138cc motor, together with TR4 type all-synchromesh gearboxes. More than 3,000 TR3Bs were sold, the last few lingering in showrooms until mid-1963. This model has given rise to confusion in the minds of some enthusiasts with the TR3 Betas, which were strictly works prototypes beyond the scope of this book. During my researches, I found one or two cryptic references to yet another model, the TR3C. Supposedly this was made in 1962 for the Canadian market, but I could find no hard evidence for the car, and it remains only a rumour. I should be interested to learn any further details.

EVOLUTION

The TRs under review can be divided into three main groups, TR2, 3 and 3A, with one further subsidiary group, the North American TR3Bs. Except for prototypes, all the cars were manufactured at Canley, Coventry, though some were exported in CKD (completely knocked down) form to various foreign countries for local assembly, and some were even supplied as chassis only, for example to Italy for Triumph Italia production. Including the TR3B run, the "sidescreen" TRs were in production for almost ten years, so inevitably there was considerable evolution in the basic design, and a great many engineering changes took place, both as regards the body and the mechanical components. This chapter will deal with the principal changes, but for reasons of space, many of the smaller modifications, particularly to engine and trim specifications, have had to be omitted. Also, Standard-Triumph's own records conflict with their published information on occasions, so certain dates and commission numbers are approximate only.

Most unusually, the TR series had commission numbers that started at Number 1 in July 1953 and continued numerically straight through to the end of TR3A production at Number 82346 in late 1961, although as mentioned elsewhere, not all numbers seem to have been used. The prefix TS, which appears to have stood merely for Triumph Sports, always appears, and the suffixes L for left-hand drive and O for overdrive as original fitments are also used. One should always be careful to distinguish a commission number ending in a final nought as part of the number, from one ending in "O" for overdrive. There is on the identification plate a gap between the last digit of the commission number itself and the "O" for overdrive, but sometimes these items get run together in registration books and similar paperwork, leading to considerable confusion. Just occasionally another suffix letter can appear; D, and DL being the most common. I have not been able to find any explanation for these. The commission number, commonly called the chassis number, is stamped on a plate rivetted to the front bulkhead under the bonnet, and is usually the best guide to the true age and identity of a car, the TR being a vehicle that was very easy to update both in appearance and in mechanical specification. Over the years, many buyers have thought that they were purchasing a TR3A only to find that behind that wide grin lurked a TR2 or 3! Today with the move to originality, this is less of a problem, but it is as well to know exactly what one possesses.

Unlike some of its contemporaries, it was possible to purchase a TR with a very basic specification at a low price, and quite a few such cars were sold, especially early in the production run. As will be seen however, a very great deal of additionsl equipment was available, and it was not uncommon for a TR to take to the road costing half as much again as the basic list price.

One thorny production problem which my researches into Standard-Triumph works files have not been able to solve is the question of what aluminium panels were fitted to the early TR2s, and for how long. Certainly the first several hundred cars had aluminium bonnets, probably up to about TS 550, and in addition aluminium spare wheel doors were fitted to early cars in roughly similar numbers. Rumours are that some of the very earliest cars also had aluminium wings and front aprons, but I have never seen evidence of this. This is quite possible however, as to get production going whilst tooling was still being delivered and supplies were being commissioned, manufacturers would sometimes resort to "Knife and Fork" methods of panel production, and this was much easier in aluminium. Throughout the run, TR engine numbers, prefixed TS and suffixed E, always ran ahead of commission numbers, as certain engines were built as spares or supplied to outside agencies, for example Morgan or Doretti. The engine number is usually therefore between 100 and 400 numbers ahead of the commission number, except on the earliest cars. No research has been done on body numbers as far as I am aware, such numbers being found on brass plates in the centre of the front bulkhead under the bonnet.

From various sources, I have been able to compile the following table of the more significant changes that occurred to the TR during its production run. It is not necessarily exhaustive, nor guaranteed accurate; one can work only within the space and from the records available!

Major change points

July 1953 TS1 and TS2 completed on 22nd July, both in

White with Geranium leather upholstery.

December 1953: From TS213, stronger handbrake assembly fitted – production now up to 25 a week.

February 1954: TS550 approximately – deletion of aluminium bonnet, substitution of steel item.

March 1954: From TS995 windscreen wiper spindle centres increased from $10^{1/2}''$ to $14^{1/2}''$ – this provides an infallible way of recognising a really early TR. Also, from engine number TS881E, the cross-drilled crankshaft was introduced.

April 1954: From TS1201, thermostat housing changed, as was the position of the radiator top outlet. At the same time, in theory at least, a new colour range was introduced, and Ice Blue, Geranium and Olive Yellow were deleted. In fact, cars in these colours were made later, well into Summer 1954 in some cases. From TS1301, new rear light assemblies fitted, incorporating reflectors, and previous separate reflectors deleted. From TS1370, an extra steering column brace was fitted.

May 1954: From TS1869 stronger road wheels fitted, $4^{1/2}J$ instead of 4J.

June 1954: From TS1927 stronger wheel nuts, retrospectively supplied to all cars. From TS1950 approximately, 24'' silencer replaced earlier (very noisy) 18'' one.

August 1954: From TS3268 battery box drain tube fitted.

September 1954: From TS3512 radiator protection cross piece introduced. From TS3514 large tenax buttons on hood replaced small ones.

October 1954: From TS4002 ''1955'' model introduced. Sill incorporated beneath the doors. From TS4229 internal bonnet release mechanism deleted, external 'DZUS' fasteners introduced.

November 1954: From TS4307 three-piece rear window in hood replaced original single piece one.

February 1955: From TS5114 revised rear hub seals. From TS5260 built in provision for fixing hardtops. From TS5348 front hubs strengthened.

March 1955: From TS5481 rear brakes increased to 10'' diameter.

April 1955: From TS6157 scuttle vent flap introduced.

May 1955: From TS6266 3-speed overdrive unit phased in, also ''Barrel'' type overdrive flick switch replaced ''pullout'' type.

October 1955: From TS8637 TR3 introduced. Revised carburettors, 2 x $1^{3/4}''$ SU H6 type, power output uprated to 95 bhp, introduction of stainless type wing bead, cellular front grille, chrome hinges for boot/bonnet (previously painted), sliding type sidescreens and other minor changes. From engine No. TS8997E camshaft bearings fitted.

November 1955: From TS9122 front lower wishbone bushes changed from rubber to nylon/steel type. From TS9350E, ''Le Mans'' type head fitted.

August 1956: From TS12606E ''High Port'' cylinder head introduced, 100 bhp (some cars still built with earlier head after this). Also, full-flow oil filter introduced.

September 1956: From TS13046 front disc brakes introduced, Girling system, together with revised, stronger rear axle. Wire wheel option now used bolt-on hub extensions, instead of different hubs as previously.

January 1957: From TS15706 two silencers fitted, instead of one with plain tailpipe.

April 1957: From engine TS18230E, chromium rocker cover specified, replacing previous painted one.

September 1957: From TS22014 revised model for 1958. Later known as TR3A, although not initially called this by Standard-Triumph. Different front apron, recessed headlights, full width grille, new type front bumper, air deflector to radiator, new stoplight arrangement, rear orange indicators, different badging, exterior lockable door handles, revised door pulls, revised seats and trim, external boot handle, and many other minor differences. New colour range.

February 1958: From TS28826 ''wedge'' type sidescreen fixings deleted, ''DZUS'' type substituted.

November 1958: From TS41878 front badge medallion now blue/white (formerly red/black). From TS42400 Ashtray fitted.

March 1959: From TS50001 different type, shorter starter motor fitted. Gearbox top cover modified – oil level plug incorporated instead of previous dipstick.

July 1959: From TS56377 rear brakes reduced from 10'' x $2^{1/4}''$ to 9'' x $1^{3/4}''$, new type of front disc brake caliper.

October 1959: From TS60001 bodyshell retooled, incorporating many detailed modifications, screen fixings changed, hinges on slightly raised platforms, rear floor pressings changed, Lucas snap connectors introduced for wiring loom. Modified petrol tank, filler cap and pipes.

December 1959: From TS64561 wiring harness changed to plastic covered wire with push-type connectors.

September 1961 (approximately): Production of TR3A finished at TS82346.

March 1962: TR3B introduced for North American market. Similar to TR3A, but commission numbers in ''TSF'' series.

May 1962: TR3B with ''TCF'' commission numbers introduced, incorporating 2138cc engine as standard, together with TR4 type all-synchromesh gearbox.

October 1962 (approximately:) Production finally ceased.

Exterior colours

TR2 August 1953 to April 1954
Geranium
Black
Pearl White
Olive Yellow
Ice Blue (in fact, more of a pale green/grey colour than blue)

TR2 May 1954 to September 1955
Black
Pearl White
British Racing Green
Signal Red
Note – Ice Blue and Geranium no longer listed, but in fact were still available until late 1954.

TR3 October 1955 to August 1957
Black
Pearl White
British Racing Green
Signal Red
Salvador Blue (replaced by Winchester Blue after December 1956)
Beige (hard-top cars only)

TR3A October 1957 to September 1961
Black
Signal Red
Pearl White (later Sebring White and finally Spa White)
British Racing Green

From March – 1958 additional colours added;
Primrose Yellow (Pale Yellow after September 1958)
Powder Blue
Pearl Grey (Silverstone Grey after September 1958)
Apple Green (available only for a brief period to special order).
The most popular colour appears to have been Signal Red, closely followed by British Racing Green and White. The least popular was the Olive Yellow on early TR2s; as far as I can trace, only 45 were built, and many were quickly resprayed, as the colour was so awful!

Factory Accessories, and optional equipment available

Overdrive, knock-on wire wheels, leather upholstery, heater, hard-top, full tool roll, telescopic steering column, Road Speed or Michelin 'X' tyres, two-speed windscreen wipers, fitted suitcase, wheeltrims for disc wheels, chromium luggage rack, tonneau cover, hood stick cover, radio set, occasional rear seat (TR3 onwards), white wall tyres, wing mirrors, licence holder for use with aeroscreens, badge bar, tailored link floor mats, ash tray, cigarette lighter, spot and fog lamps, reversing lamp, screen washer kit.

Competition and speed equipment available (from factory)

Cast aluminium engine sump, 4.1 to 1 rear axle (TR3A), 2138cc engine (TR3A), competition suspension, aeroscreens, undershield, rear wheel spats, metal cockpit cover, anti roll bar (from TR3A), Alfin brake drums, competition brake linings, radiator skid shield.

SPECIFICATION

Specifications – TR2, TR3, TR3A, TR3B

Type code
20 TR2, 20 TR3 from October 1955.

Built
Prototypes – Standard-Triumph experimental department, Banner Lane, Coventry.
Production Cars – Standard-Triumph Works, Canley Coventry, Warwickshire.
Bodies built by Mulliners Limited, Birmingham.
Chassis frames by Standard-Triumph to TS1401, thereafter by Sankey & Co.

Numbers built
TR2 production
August 1953 to August/September 1955.
Commencing at commission number TS1.
Finishing at commission number TS8636.
Total built 8628 (a few numbers from the sequence appear not to have been used).

TR3 production
Commencing at commission number TS8637, September/October, 1955.
Finishing at commission number TS22013, September 1957.
Total built 13376 (believed all numbers actually used).

TR3A production
(Note – car not referred to initially as TR3A by manufacturers, TR3 designation still utilised).
Commencing at commission number TS22014, October 1957.
Finishing at commission number TS82346, September 1961.
Total built 58250 approximately (note – not all numbers were used – there is a considerable gap in numbering in the TS48XXX and TS49XXX series, with very little evidence that cars bearing these numbers were actually made – in addition, certain other numbers appear not to have been used).

TR3B production (North America only)
Commencing March 1962, TSF1 to TSF530
Commencing May, 1962 TCF1 to TCF2804 (both believed fully

consecutive)

Production ceased October 1962 approximately – total TR3Bs built – 3334.

Note: 'L' suffix to commission number indicates Left-hand drive.
'O' suffix indicates overdrive fitted from new.

Configuration – TR2	Front engine, manual transmission with optional overdrive, rear wheel drive, 2-seater open sports body, with optional hardtop (from October 1954).
Engine – TR2	Developed from Standard Vanguard and Ferguson tractor engine, produced by Standard Motor Company. Four cylinder, wet-liner configuration, water-cooled cast-iron block and cylinder head. Push rod operated overhead valves. Single camshaft mounted in block.
Bore	83mm (3.268 inches)
Stroke	92mm (3.622 inches)
Displacement	1991 c.c. (121.5 cubic inches)
Compression ratio	8.5 to 1.
Maximum power	90 bhp at 4800 r.p.m.
Maximum torque	117.5 lbf ft at 3000 r.p.m.
Carburettors	2 x H4 1$\frac{1}{2}$'' SU semi-downdraught carburettors with 'pancake' air filters with AC type 'UE' camshaft driven mechanical fuel pump.
Engine oil capacity	11 pints (from dry) – 6.25 litres.
Cooling system	13 pints (14 with heater fitted) normal running temperature 85°C (185°F)
Gearbox	Floor mounted gear lever controlling four-speed and reverse gear box, the top three speeds fitted with synchromesh. Optional overdrive available (Laycock-de-Normanville type), electrically controlled from dashboard. Initially overdrive operating on top gear only, but later cars having overdrive on 2nd, 3rd and 4th gears (TS6266 onwards).
Oil capacity from dry	1$\frac{1}{2}$ pints – non overdrive gearbox (0.8 litres) 3$\frac{1}{2}$ pints – overdrive gearbox (2.0 litres)
Gear ratios	1st 3.38 2nd 2.00 2nd overdrive 1.64 3rd 1.325 3rd overdrive 1.086 Top 1.00 Top overdrive 0.82 Reverse 4.28
Clutch	Borg and Beck single dry plate clutch, 9 inch diameter, hydraulically operated.
Rear axle	Hypoid bevel semi-floating type, ratio 3.7 to 1. Oil capacity 1$\frac{1}{2}$ pints (0.8 litres). Hardy-Spicer propeller shaft.

Overall gear ratios	1st 12.5	
	2nd 7.4	2nd overdrive 6.07
	3rd 4.9	3rd overdrive 4.02
	Top 3.7	Top overdrive 3.03

Road speed at 1000 RPM (based on original 5.50 x 15 crossply tyres)

Overdrive Top	24.6 mph
Top	20.2 mph
Overdrive Third	18.5 mph
Third	15.2 mph
Overdrive Second	12.3 mph
Second	10.1 mph
First	6.00 mph

Engine revolutions at 100 mph (allowing for tyre growth at speed, crossply tyres)
4800 rpm in direct top
3900 rpm in overdrive top

Chassis

Box section frame, with longitudinal side members, tubular outrigger body supports, 2 front and 2 rear crossmembers with cruciform central cross bracing.

Steering Gear

Adjustable cam and lever type, ratio 12 to 1, with 3 piece track rod. $2^1/3$ turns lock to lock, turning circle 32 feet left, 31 feet right (telescopic steering column optional).

Suspension

Front

Independent with upper and lower wishbone arms with coil springs; telescopic dampers within the front springs. No anti-roll bar (available later as an option).

Rear

Semi elliptic rear springs, damped by Armstrong lever-arm shock-absorbers. No other control.

Brakes

Lockheed system hydraulically operated, two leading shoe front brakes, 10'' diameter by $2^1/4$'' width, rear brakes initially 9'' diameter by $1^3/4$'' width, but increased to 10'' diameter by $2^1/4$'' width from car number TS5481. Cable operated mechanical handbrake on the rear wheels.

Wheels and tyres

15 inch steel wheels, perforated for cooling, initially 4'' rims, later increased to $4^1/2$''. Tyres 5.50 x 15 crossply (later 5.90 x 15). Wire wheels, 48 spoke with knock-on hubs available as optional extras. Standard pressure 22 lbf/in² front, 24 lbf/in² rear. Dunlop Road Speed tyres available for high speed at extra cost.

Bodywork

Styled by Walter Belgrove, and designed to keep tooling costs to the absolute minimum, the body featured as many bolt-on panels as possible, which facilitated easier repair and renovation. Open 2 seater, cut-away doors, all steel construction (initially bonnet and spare-wheel door of aluminium). Optional glass-fibre or steel hardtops available. Full weather equipment with removable sidescreens with signalling flaps (2 pane sliding type with hard top). Optional tonneau cover, removable windscreen, optional aeroscreens. Vynide seat facings and trim, with leather as optional extra (standard on very early cars).

Electrical system	12 volt, positive earth with single 51 amp hour, 12 volt battery mounted centrally under the bonnet on bulkhead. Lucas C39 Dynamo, Lucas M418G starter, Lucas DM2 distributor, Lucas RB106 control box/regulator, Twin Lucas WT614/618 Horns, Lucas CRT15 wiper motor, Lucas double dip 60/36 watt headlights, type F700 pre-focus, Lucas flashing direction indicators, combined with side/tail lamps. Lucas 525 single, central stoplamp.

Main dimensions

Overall length	12ft 7'' (3m 84cm)
Overall width	4ft 7$\frac{1}{2}$'' (1m 41cm)
Height (hood up)	4ft 2$\frac{1}{2}$'' (1m 28cm)
Height of scuttle	3ft 4'' (1m 02cm)
Wheelbase	7ft 4'' (2m 24cm)
Front track	3ft 9'' (1m 14cm)
Rear track	3ft 9$\frac{1}{2}$'' (1m 16cm)
Ground clearance	6'' (15.2 cm)
Dry weight (for shipping)	1981 lbs (902kg)
Kerb weight in running order	2107 lbs (955kg)
Fuel tank	12$\frac{1}{2}$ gallons capacity

Performance TR2 (representative of all models) with Hood and sidescreens in place –

Max speed	107 mph
Max in third	76 mph (at 5000 rpm)
Max in second	51 mph (at 5000 rpm)
Max in first	30 mph (at 5000 rpm)
Acceleration	0 – 60 mph 11.9 seconds
	0 – 90 mph 30.5 seconds
	standing $\frac{1}{4}$ mile 18.6 seconds
Fuel consumption	32 mpg overall approximately (28 mpg for TR3/3A/3B)

Note: removal of windscreen and substitution of aeroscreen can increase top speed to 112/114 mph

TR3 series

As TR2 except for the following	Type Code 20TR3

Engine

Maximum power	95 bhp (early ''Le Mans'' type ''low-port'' head)
	100 bhp (Later ''high-port'' head)
	Carburettor 2 x H6 1$\frac{3}{4}$'' SUs.

Rear Axle	As TR2 up to TS13045, but much stronger rear axle with Girling brakes fitted from TS13046.
Brakes	As TR2 up to TS13045, but front disc brakes by Girling fitted from TS13046, 11 inch discs, no servo, with 10 x 2$\frac{1}{4}$ Girling rear brakes.
Bodywork	Introduction of cellular front grille, sliding sidescreens and stainless steel wing beading.
Wheels and Tyres	Michelin 'X' steel braced radials available as optional extras, 155 x 15.
TR3A Series	As TR3 except for the following:-
Engine	86mm bore, 2138cc engine became available as optional extra in 1959. Compression ratio 9 to 1.

Rear Axle	4.1 to 1 ratio axle became available as an alternative to the standard 3.7 to 1 (4.1 to 1 supplied with overdrive only).
Brakes	From TS56377 new type Girling calipers introduced for front discs, and rear brakes reduced in size to 9" to 1$^3/_4$".
Bodywork	New front apron panel, recessed headlights, redesigned front bumper and grille, exterior door handles and boot handle, separate indicator lamps at rear, redesigned seats and other minor differences.
TR3B March to October 1962	"TSF" series as final TR3As, but "TCF" series fitted as standard with 2138cc engine and TR4 type all synchromesh four speed gearbox.

ROAD TESTS

The **Motor**

354

April 7, 1954

The **Motor** Road Test No. 12/54 (Continental)—

Make: Triumph **Type:** T.R.2. Sports 2-seater (with overdrive)
Makers: The Standard Motor Co. Ltd., Coventry.

Test Data

CONDITIONS: Cold, dry weather with moderate cross wind. Belgian premium-grade pump fuel. Smooth concrete road surface (Ostend-Ghent motor road). Car tested with hood and sidescreens erect, and with tyre pressures at 28-32 lb. as advised for sustained high speeds.

INSTRUMENTS
Speedometer at 30 m.p.h.	4% fast
Speedometer at 60 m.p.h.	5% fast
Speedometer at 90 m.p.h.	6% fast
Distance recorder	1% fast

MAXIMUM SPEEDS
Flying Quarter Mile (overdrive gear)
Mean of four opposite runs	107.3 m.p.h.
Best time equals	108.4 m.p.h.

Speed in gears
Max. speed in 4th gear	105.3 m.p.h.
Max. speed in 3rd gear	79 m.p.h.
Max. speed in 2nd gear	52 m.p.h.
Max. speed in 1st gear	31 m.p.h.

FUEL CONSUMPTION (in overdrive)
52.0 m.p.g. at constant 30 m.p.h.	
54.0 m.p.g. at constant 40 m.p.h.	
49.5 m.p.g. at constant 50 m.p.h.	
43.5 m.p.g. at constant 60 m.p.h.	
37.5 m.p.g. at constant 70 m.p.h.	
31.0 m.p.g. at constant 80 m.p.h.	
27.0 m.p.g. at constant 90 m.p.h.	

Overall consumption for 1,904 miles, 55.2 gallons, 34.5 m.p.g. Fuel tank capacity 12½ gallons.

ACCELERATION TIMES Through Gears
0-30 m.p.h.	4.0 sec.
0-40 m.p.h.	6.0 sec.
0-50 m.p.h.	8.2 sec.
0-60 m.p.h.	12.0 sec.
0-70 m.p.h.	15.8 sec.
0-80 m.p.h.	22.1 sec.
0-90 m.p.h.	30.4 sec.
Standing Quarter Mile	18.6 sec.

ACCELERATION TIMES on Three Upper Ratios
	Overdrive Top	4th	3rd
10-30 m.p.h	—	8.6 sec.	6.0 sec.
20-40 m.p.h	11.0 sec.	8.6 sec.	5.8 sec.
30-50 m.p.h	11.3 sec.	8.7 sec.	6.0 sec.
40-60 m.p.h	12.5 sec.	9.0 sec.	6.5 sec.
50-70 m.p.h	14.2 sec.	10.1 sec.	7.0 sec.
60-80 m.p.h	16.0 sec.	11.3 sec.	—
70-90 m.p.h	19.3 sec.	14.2 sec.	—

WEIGHT
Unladen Kerb Weight	18¾ cwt.
Front/rear weight distribution	54 46
Weight laden as tested	22¼ cwt.

HILL CLIMBING in 4th gear (At steady speeds).
Max. speed on 1 in 20	94 m.p.h. (overdrive 82 m.p.h.)
Max. speed on 1 in 15	89 m.p.h. (overdrive 69 m.p.h.)
Max. speed on 1 in 10	71 m.p.h.
Max. gradient on overdrive gear	1 in 11.4 (Tapley 195 lb. ton.)
Max. gradient on 4th gear	1 in 8.0 (Tapley 275 lb. ton.)
Max. gradient on 3rd gear	1 in 5.9 (Tapley 375 lb. ton.)

BRAKES at 30 m.p.h.
1.00 g retardation	30 ft. stopping distance with 135 lb. pedal pressure.
0.97 g retardation	31 ft. stopping distance with 100 lb. pedal pressure.
0.70 g retardation	43 ft. stopping distance with 75 lb. pedal pressure.
0.42 g retardation	72 ft. stopping distance with 50 lb. pedal pressure.
0.22 g retardation	137 ft. stopping distance with 25 lb. pedal pressure.

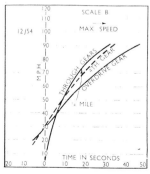

Drag at 10 m.p.h.	29 lb.
Drag at 60 m.p.h.	112 lb.

Specific fuel consumption when cruising at 80%, of maximum speed (i.e. 85.8 m.p.h.) on level road, based on power delivered to rear wheels .. 0.59 pints per b.h.p./hr.

Maintenance

Sump: 11 pints, S.A.E. 30 summer, S.A.E. 20 winter. **Gearbox:** 1½ pints, S.A.E. 30 (2 pints extra on overdrive models). **Rear Axle:** 1½ pints S.A.E. 90 hypoid gear oil. **Steering gear:** S.A.E. 90 gear oil. **Radiator:** 13 pints (2 drain taps). **Chassis lubrication:** By grease gun every 1,000 miles to 13 points and every 5,000 miles to 10 additional points. **Ignition timing:** 4° B.T.D.C. static. **Spark plug gap:** 0.032 in. **Contact breaker gap:** 0.015 in. **Valve timing** (set with 0.015 in. valve clearance): Inlet opens 15° B.T.D.C.; Exhaust closes 15° A.T.D.C. **Tappet clearances:** (Cold). Inlet 0.010 in. Exhaust 0.012 in. (for high speeds, 0.013 in., inlet and exhaust). **Front wheel toe-in:** ⅛ in. **Camber angle:** 2° positive. **Castor angle:** 1-2° positive. **Tyre pressures** (normal use): Front 22 lb. Rear 24 lb. (increase by 6-8 lb. for sustained high speeds). **Brake fluid:** Lockheed orange. **Battery:** 12-volt. 51 amp.-hr., Lucas GTW9A 2. **Lamp bulbs:** 12 volt. **Headlamps:** 60/36 watt Lucas No. 404. **Parking, tail and number plate lamps,** 18/6 watt Lucas No. 361.

Ref. B/20/54

April 7, 1954   355   *THE MOTOR*

The TRIUMPH SPORTS
(With Overdrive)

The Lowest-priced British 100 m.p.h. Car Displays Astonishing Fuel Economy

LOW FRONTAL AREA gives minimum air resistance but leaves useful internal roominess. High-mounted headlamps have a useful range but give a very limited sideways spread of light.

In Brief	
Price (with overdrive) £635 (plus purchase tax £265 14s. 2d.) equals £900 14s. 2d.	
Capacity	1,991 c.c.
Unladen kerb weight ...	18½ cwt.
Fuel consumption... ...	34.5 m.p.g.
Maximum speed ...	107.3 m.p.h.
Maximum speed on 1 in 20 gradient...	94 m.p.h. (4th gear)
Maximum top (4th) gear gradient...	1 in 8.0
Acceleration:	
10-30 m.p.h. in top (4th)	8.6 secs.
0-50 m.p.h. through gears	8.2 secs.
Gearing: 20.2 m.p.h. in top (4th) at 1,000 r.p.m. (24.6 m.p.h. in overdrive); 83.5 m.p.h. at 2,500 ft. per min. piston speed (102 m.p.h. in overdrive).	

IN BRITAIN and also in many important export markets, the Triumph T.R.2 sports two-seater which we have recently tested over a distance of 2,000 miles is much the lowest-priced car which can exceed the "magic" speed of 100 m.p.h. Equipped with the manually selected overdrive fifth gear ratio which is an optional extra, it is also a car whose fuel economy verges upon the fantastic.

Engine, transmission and body designers have combined with unusual effectiveness to give this roomy two-seater car its remarkable performance, highlights of which are the ability to accelerate from rest to 60 m.p.h. in only 12 seconds, a maximum speed (with hood and sidescreens erect) of 107.3 m.p.h., and fuel consumption figures which range from 54 m.p.g. at a steady 40 m.p.h. to 27 m.p.g. at a steady 90 m.p.h. Reasonable all-up weight has been combined with very low air resistance to make this an easy-running car, and a highly efficient engine has been combined with extremely advantageous gearing to provide astonishing economy of fuel. It requires emphasis that our measured performance

figures were no flash-in-the-pan, but were recorded on the way back from a visit to Switzerland without any attention being given to tappets, sparking plugs, contact breaker or other engine details for more than 1,500 miles.

Derived from the well-tried Standard Vanguard engine, the power unit of the Triumph Sports has a reduced cylinder bore which brings its size just below 2 litres, pistons giving reduced friction, a high compression cylinder head, and two S.U. carburetters. The compression ratio of 8½/1 is high enough to allow the engine to pink at low speeds on any premium-grade fuel which we tried, but neither the high compression ratio nor the modified valve timing and dual carburetters which permit higher r.p.m. to be attained have robbed the engine of its known ability to pull well at moderate speeds. An instant starter from cold, it develops enough power to give the car excellent performance when using extremely economical carburetter settings.

Delightful Gearbox

The gearbox and overdrive which have been mated to this engine are, for the keen driver, a sheer delight. The four-speed gearbox, which is controlled by a sturdy and nicely positioned central remote-control lever, has the close ratios which are expected on a sports car and synchromesh mechanism which is amply effective without being obstructive. A push-pull electrical switch engages and disengages the overdrive (which operates only when top gear is in use) positively and reasonably smoothly without use of the clutch. No automatic or semi-automatic device is

provided to take over from the keen driver the pleasant duty of deciding for himself which of the five progressively spaced gear ratios he wants to use at any particular moment. To complete the transmission, there is a clutch which is firm-acting without being so fierce as to preclude starts from rest in 2nd gear, and a hypoid rear axle which allows 100 m.p.h. to be exceeded even without use of the optional-extra overdrive ratio. This car has the pleasing characteristic of being free from "awkward speeds," of being able to produce good acceleration in one ratio or another at any pace between a standstill and 90 m.p.h. or more.

The overdrive gear fitted to the test car is an optional but extremely worth-while extra, omission of which reduces the basic price by £40 and saves a further £16 13s. 4d. on purchase tax in the case of home-market sales. Using the direct 4th ratio instead of the overdrive 5th gear only reduced the timed maximum speed from 107.3 m.p.h. to 105.3 m.p.h., but the former figure corresponds to something less than the recommended limit for sustained engine speed of 4,500 r.p.m., whereas the latter figure is attained with an engine speed of approximately 5,250 r.p.m.

CUT-AWAY DOORS have their tops padded to form comfortable elbow rests. The tonneau cover has a central zip-fastener, so that it can be used to cover one half, three-quarters or the whole of the cockpit.

FULL INSTRUMENTATION is provided, with the speedometer and "rev. counter" directly facing the driver. Other details visible in these pictures are separately adjustable seats, fly-off handbrake, central remote-control gear-lever, and push-pull overdrive switch on the right of the facia panel.

The Triumph Sports - - Contd.

Brake performance fully adequate to make the use of high speeds safe on the road has been provided on this model, which has 10-inch front and 9-inch rear brakes. The optional wire-spoke wheels would no doubt provide improved brake cooling for racing, but in normal form the car can be braked from high speed without any judder or sideways pull, and can be driven uncomplainingly down an Alpine pass in top gear. The "hanging" type pedals which go with hydraulic brake and clutch operation seem more than usually comfortable with the "straight legs" driving position of a low-built sports car, there being no inconvenient sloping toe-board to restrict heel movement. To the left of the clutch, the driver's foot rests naturally on the dip-switch. Effective in use, the fly-off pattern handbrake is so placed that it can chafe the driver's left calf.

Bodywork Details

Simple and rather unconventional in outline, the body lines of the Triumph evoke varied reactions from different people the same may be said concerning the "geranium" paintwork of the model submitted for test. From a practical point of view, the merit of the bodywork shaping is unquestionable, there being comfortable room for two people and a fair amount of loose luggage inside the car, and a surprising amount of further luggage room in the rear locker, despite which the air resistance of the car with its hood and sidescreens erect is notably low. Like most open cars, this one loses some of its maximum speed when the hood is folded, an effective windscreen being also quite an effective airbrake, but for racing the complete windscreen can very easily be removed from the car and replaced by aero-screens.

Driven in cool spring sunshine with the hood folded but the sidescreens in position and the tonneau cover blanking off the space behind the seats, this model is certainly no more cold or draughty than most other open cars. Our test model had the optional-extra interior heater and windscreen de-mister fitted, this providing useful warmth around the legs even with the hood lowered and being able to keep the interior very snug when the hood is raised.

Two adjustable bucket seats are provided, but they fall just short of desirable comfort standards. For driving to Switzerland and back, we found that a thin rubber cushion which made up for inadequate padding over the seat springs also raised the driving position sufficiently to eliminate a "blind spot" behind the rear-view mirror, without cramping headroom below the hood for an average driver. Much care has obviously gone into details of the hood, the rubberised canvas of which removes completely from a folding frame, this unit being easily and quite reasonably quickly raised or lowered single-handed and behaving well during fast driving. A full-length tonneau cover, providing protection against rain showers or casual pilfering when the open car is parked, forms part of the normal equipment. With the hood erect, rearward vision is good, and with the car open all-round vision is of course virtually 100% clear.

At present, certain annoyances result from details of the body design, and it must be hoped that these will soon be dealt with. Extending the doors down several inches below floor level results in it being impossible to open one door when the car is parked beside the kerb in a majority of city streets. The absence of exterior door-handles, and of easy means of securing or releasing from inside the car the useful elbow-flaps in the rigid-framed sidescreens,

plus the fact that a key (different from the ignition key) must always be used to open or close a capacious locker on the facia panel, are at present major irritants on a car which is in most respects perfectly suitable for year-round everyday use. A vital point of merit with this open body is that under no circumstances do exhaust fumes appear to get sucked forwards into the cockpit.

With its comfortable body, considerable luggage capacity, high performance and astonishing economy of fuel, the Triumph comes close to being a magnificent vehicle for long-distance continental travel on business or on pleasure. At this early stage in the model's life, however (the example tested had engine no. 9 in chassis no. 6), chassis qualities which are very adequate for countries such as Britain with reasonably smooth roads, proved disappointing on the fast and bumpy roads of France and Belgium.

With the 22-24 lb. tyre pressures suggested for normal use, the Triumph rides very comfortably at touring-car speeds. There is none of the traditional sports-car harshness, but there is a certain amount of roll and a good deal of tyre squeal during fast cornering. For our performance tests and most of our other driving, the Dunlop "Road Speed" tyres which are optional extra equipment had their inflation pressures increased by 6 lb. sq. in., as is

TWIN CARBURETTERS and modified valve timing are among the specification changes which allow a well-tried engine to provide sporting performance on a very low fuel consumption. Under-bonnet accessibility is commendably good.

Mechanical Specification

Engine

Cylinders	4
Bore and Stroke	83 mm. x 92 mm.
Cubic capacity	1,991 c.c.
Piston area	33.5 sq. in.
Valves	Pushrod o.h.v.
Compression ratio	8.5/1
Max. power 90 b.h.p.	at 4,800 r.p.m.
Piston speed at max. b.h.p.	2,900 ft. per min.
Carburetters	2 S.U. inclined, Type H.4
Ignition	12-volt coil
Sparking plugs	14 mm. Champion L10S
	(For hard driving, type L11S)
Fuel pump	AC mechanical
Oil filter	Purolator by-pass

Transmission

Clutch	Borg & Beck 9-in. s.d.p.
Overdrive (clutchless engagement)	3.03
Top gear (s/m)	3.7
3rd gear (s/m)	4.9
2nd gear (s/m)	7.4
1st gear	12.5
Propeller shaft	Hardy Spicer open
Final drive	Hypoid bevel
Top gear, m.p.h. at 1,000 r.p.m.	20.2
(Overdrive, 24.6)	
Top gear, m.p.h. at 1,000 ft/min. piston speed 33.4	(Overdrive, 40.8)

Chassis

Brakes	Lockheed hydraulic
Brake drums	Front, 10 in. x 2¼ in.
	Rear, 9 in. x 1¾ in.
Friction lining area	148 sq. in.
Suspension Front	Coil and wishbone i.f.s.
Rear	Semi-elliptic
Shock absorbers Front	Telescopic
Rear	Piston-type
Tyres	Dunlop 5.50—15
	(Road Speed type on test car)

Steering

Steering gear	Cam and lever
Turning circle: Left	32 feet
Right	30 feet
Turns of steering wheel, lock to lock	2¾

Performance factors (at laden weight as tested):

Piston area, sq. in. per ton	30.1
Brake lining area, sq. in. per ton	133
Specific displacement, litres per ton mile 2,660	(Overdrive, 2,180)

Fully described in "The Motor" October 22, 1952

Coachwork and Equipment

Bumper height with car unladen:	
Front	(max.) 17½ in., (min.) 9½ in.
Rear (2 vertical bars only)	
	(max.) 20½ in., (min.) 11½ in.
Starting handle	Yes
Battery mounting	On scuttle
Jack	Screw type
Jacking points	On frame, reached through trap-doors in floor
Tool kit:	Wheelbrace, jack, starting handle.
Exterior lights:	Two headlamps, two side lamps/direction indicators, two tail lamps/direction indicators, one stop/number plate lamp.
Direction indicators	Flashing type, self-cancelling
Windscreen wipers	Two-blade electric
Instruments:	Speedometer with decimal trip, tachometer, oil pressure gauge, coolant thermometer, ammeter, fuel contents gauge.
Warning lights:	Dynamo charge, headlamp main beam, direction indicators.
Locks: With ignition key	Ignition
With other key	Glove locker, luggage boot
Glove lockers	One on facia, with locking lid
Map pockets	Two on doors
Parcel shelves	Nil
Ashtrays	Nil
Cigar lighters	Nil
Interior lights	Nil
Interior heater:	Optional extra, re-circulating type, with windscreen de-misters.
Car radio	Optional extra
Extras available:	Overdrive, knock-on wire wheels, cast aluminium engine sump, stiffer front springs, larger rear shock absorbers, aero-screens, undershield, rear wing spats, leather upholstery, metal cockpit cover, interior heater, radio, tool roll and tools, telescopic steering column, Road Speed tyres, two-speed screen wipers, fitted suitcase, dished steering wheel.
Upholstery material	Vynide
Floor covering	Pile carpets
Exterior colours standardized (with effect from May, 1954):	Signal red, pearl white, British racing green, black. Upholstery: Brown, blue or red. Hood and sidescreens: Fawn or black.

advised for sustained high speed driving, this also giving quicker steering response.

Over virtually the whole range of lateral accelerations used on sharp or moderately large-radius corners, this car shows a consistent but not exaggerated "understeer" characteristic, so that it is viceless right up to the limit of tyre adhesion. Only on wet and slippery roads did raised tyre inflation pressures appear to impair road-holding qualities. On really fast curves, however, it is wise to allow for the fact that due to light damping of the rear springs an unex-

LUGGAGE ACCOMMODATION inside the car is supplemented by an external locker of useful size which may be locked with either Yale or carriage keys. A separate lower compartment accommodates the spare wheel and jack.

pected bump can throw the car off its line to some extent. At speed, the steering is direct enough to transmit a fair amount of reaction to the driver's hands.

Especially with the car laden with two people and their normal touring luggage, the standard suspension seems much too lightly damped for open but badly surfaced roads, so that it can be necessary to keep the cruising speed down to 70 m.p.h. or less in circumstances when a much higher pace would otherwise be safe and economical. Unhappily, the exhaust system at present in use emits a quite ludi-

rous amount of noise at engine speeds around 2,400 r.p.m., and in the overdrive gear this often corresponds closely to natural cruising speeds used at night or on rough roads.

It will be noted that, amongst the items of optional equipment available for this model, stiffer front springs and larger rear shock absorbers are listed, and the latter at least are probably desirable for long-distance travel as well as for racing use. Increased damping would also no doubt minimize unexpectedly vigorous "shake" of the front end and scuttle at speeds around 75-80 m.p.h. which became increasingly evident towards the end of our extended Continental test, although the impression is formed that further stiffening of the frame or scuttle may be desirable.

Apart from chassis imperfections on this early example, the Triumph has merit for fast business travel as well as for sporting use. Almost completely weatherproof, even if slightly undignified to enter when the hood is raised, its astonishing economy at fast cruising speeds is backed up by the provision of a large fuel tank which enabled us to drive quite rapidly from Geneva to Calais, over 450 miles away, without any re-fuelling stop. Secured by two locks instead of the usual one, the alligator bonnet gives very good access to the power unit. The light and high-geared steering provides an extremely compact turning circle. A full set of instruments has been sensibly arranged on the plastic-covered facia panel.

Although we have felt obliged to criticize some details and characteristics of the Triumph T.R.2 Sports two-seater in quite emphatic terms, we nevertheless rate this as not merely the best sports car available at its price, but also as one of the most promising new models which has been introduced in recent years. Not pared down to minimum weight especially with a view to use as a competition car, this model offers a combination of comfort, economy, speed and sheer enjoyment of travel in a responsive open two-seater, which should assure it of very large sales in many parts of the world.

IMPRESSIONS OF THE TRIUMPH TR2

A British Sports Car that is Practical, Economical and Represents Excellent Value-for-Money

TO review our road experiences with a Triumph TR2 for the benefit of the large number of potential buyers of these cars is not as easy as it might seem.

The TR2 is by now a well-established sports model, and to describe it as a very good one is to state the obvious, after the splendid showing in competition motoring by this Coventry-product which, after all, is a skilful development of standard components and not a specialised sports car designed for such tasks. Further, so many satisfied owners of these cars meet and discuss their virtues and shortcomings that a full test-report of the TR2 would be repetitive ground.

However, although this car has come to us for review rather late, we are convinced, from the many inquiries we receive as to its character and manner-of-going, that some impressions will be acceptable to the majority of our readers.

Before embarking on this task, let us get the sports Triumph in proper perspective. Design of the TR2 was commenced in about March, 1952, and the first production example was exhibited at the Earls Court Motor Show of that year.

The idea was to meet the growing demand for a compact, fast and not-too-expensive two-seater of modern lines and this the Triumph design-team did with some skill, by using a Standard Eight chassis, with Triumph Mayflower axle and suspension units, powered by the trusty Standard Vanguard engine linered-down from 2,088 c.c. to under 2 litres and endowed with a new cylinder-head to take two carburetters. The Vanguard four-cylinder long-stroke wet-liner engine was a " safe bet " for the job, for it had already proved its reliability and freedom from servicing snags in tractors and the versatile Vanguard saloon, besides being employed by the Morgan Motor Company in single-carburetter 68-b.h.p. form to power their Plus Four sports car.

The developed engine gave 75 b.h.p., was mated to a modified Vanguard gearbox providing four forward speeds, and gave the 1952 TR2 a maximum speed of 90 m.p.h.

The immense and immediate interest which this new Triumph aroused caused the Company to swiftly iron out the initial bugs. They improved the shape of the tail, stiffened the frame, fitted an overdrive gear and increased the power output to 90 b.h.p. It is to Standard's everlasting credit that, having come thus far, instead of sitting back to admire, they sent their test-driver, K. Richardson, to Lindley, where he was set to lap the M.I.R.A. track for hour after hour at over 100 m.p.h. The chassis proved satisfactorily stable, but the hard-tried engine flung big-ends and broke its exhaust valves. Valuable lessons were learnt and the production TR2 was soon able to present itself as a 100 m.p.h. two-seater of modest first-cost, surprising economy and freed of earlier weaknesses.

Since then we need hardly remind our readers that a special

version has reached 125 m.p.h. at Jabbeke, and others have finished in the Mille Miglia and Le Mans races and performed outstandingly in their class in the T.T., while the rally successes of the TR2 are legion.

It is now our happy task to present our personal, detailed impressions of a normal 1954 wire-wheeled TR2 which came along for test just before Christmas and which, at this hardly ideal time of year, covered a four-figure mileage in the hands of various members of the staff, to their general complete satisfaction.

The makers had requested us not to submit the car to a full road-test ritual and consequently no performance figures were recorded. The abilities of the TR2 are by now well known, so it suffices to say that the engine ran up to a limit of 5,000 r.p.m., with only slight vibration towards peak speed to reveal it as a four-cylinder power unit. In top 100 m.p.h. (5,000 r.p.m.) calls for favourable conditions. A very easy indicated 95 m.p.h. is obtainable, with a few more m.p.h. coming up along normal clear stretches of highway. On good roads, at this pace the Triumph has a commendably straight path—it is perfectly happy at upwards of 90 on the speedometer. The car we tested had wire wheels shod with ordinary Dunlop tyres.

Acceleration is vivid, to express oneself mildly, and third gear sufficiently close to top to be useful, although the other ratios are somewhat low. The exhaust note is rather prominent, while speed is thus rapidly increased, but in top gear the car is unobtrusive. If completely quiet negotiation of a town or village is called for, over-drive top is the gear to employ.

Overdrive, with its convenient control-button, endows the TR2 with the effect of having, with its tractor-like torque-curve, a five-speed gearbox. As the engine is willing to pull the high (3.03 to 1) o/d ratio from 1,500 r.p.m. upwards, this is normally employed, a rapid change being possible into normal top (or fourth speed) by operation of the aforesaid button, so useful for overtaking fast-cruising traffic, as 500 r.p.m. is gained on the power curve. The highest speed achieved was an indicated 112 m.p.h. (3,900 r.p.m.) equal to a calculated 97 m.p.h., whereas in fourth gear the highest indicated speed was 100 m.p.h.

For a car with a basic price of only £625, the speed and acceleration are beyond criticism and of high merit. Besides the performance of the TR2 (which, as we proved, enables a jaunt from London to Exeter and back again to be fitted in comfortably between morning coffee and a late dinner, taking lunch en route and never fully extending the car) its other qualities are astonishing for so modest a purchase price.

The body is comfortable, and snug when the hood and screens are erect, the ride is comfortable, and the controls pleasant to handle. If the outward appearance of the TR2 still leaves a good deal to be desired, the interior appointments are for the most part practical, pleasing and of good quality.

The instruments are sensibly grouped, with the 5-in. Jaeger speedometer and rev.-counter in front of the driver and only very mildly masked by the three-spoke, spring steering wheel. On the centre panel are separate dials showing oil pressure (normally a healthy 60 lb./sq. in.), water temperature (mostly 185 deg. F.), petrol contents and dynamo charge. These dials have black faces with white lettering and as unobtrusive recorders in good taste, convenient to read, could hardly be bettered. The rev.-counter needle is remarkably steady; the speedometer reads to 120 m.p.h. and incorporates trip and total mileage recorders. The panel lighting is over-bright, but the dynamo warning light is tolerable. That for the direction-indicators, however, is not only too bright but flashes in unison ! The speedometer has a full-headlamps-beam indicator-light which, it so happens, enables the welcome outline of the speedo-meter needle to be seen at night, when the panel lights have been extinguished. There is no clock.

The minor control-buttons are likewise black with white lettering, of good quality, especially the push-in starter-button, but so grouped that those controlling lamps, wipers and panel lighting are set one above the other, leading to confusion of the gloved hand at night. Moreover, we do not love the pull-out combined head and side-lamps switch. The overdrive-button is very conveniently set for operation by the right hand and beside it is the heater-knob, its on-off action a thought indecisive.

FOR REVIEW.— The Triumph TR2 driven for a four-figure mileage by MOTOR SPORT. It possessed wire wheels, heater and overdrive, and the old-style doors.

Full marks for the heater fitted to the TR2, which sends a fine volume of warm air over one's feet and lower-half, so useful in an open car, and which can be easily regulated from the single knob, the heat released on one or both sides of the cockpit by the use of flaps, or the flow of water turned off by an under-bonnet valve for ventilation in summer.

The screen is large, inclined and solidly mounted, providing excellent protection without promoting dazzle, and, most commendably, is of laminated glass. The screen-wipers function well, working in unison, but would benefit from water-squirts, and neither they, nor the heater, can be used unless the ignition is switched on. There are heater outlets behind the screen, and the back of the bonnet-top is slotted to direct hot air onto the screen face.

Before the passenger there is a generous, lidded cubby-hole, but a key is required to open it and this can only be withdrawn after the lid has been shut, which is unnecessarily complicated.

The entire body gives the impression of being well made and it is virtually free from noises, except for a prominent rattle from the passenger's door. The doors shut well and possess usefully commodious rigid pockets. On the car tested they fouled high knobs when opened and there are no outside handles, which is somewhat inconvenient when the sidescreens are erect. The inside handles are worked by " pulls," the attachment screws of which take a considerable load, and to reach these with the sidescreens up zip fasteners are provided in the screens.

The separate, adjustable bucket seats provide a big range of adjustment, easily effected, and are quite comfortable, although considerably more support of back and shoulders would be a decided improvement and the cushions are just a little on the hard side.

The pedals are badly placed for a heel-and-toe gear-change, and set to the offside of the steering column; those for clutch and brake are rather loosely hung, but convenient to the feet. The interior of the cockpit is carpeted and there is a rubber pad where the passenger's left toe might rub. The seats and dash are Vynide-covered and the body-sides nicely padded. The gearbox and transmission tunnel is not so big that the clutch-foot cannot find anywhere to rest; there is ample room, although a stronger spring for the foot headlamps-dimmer would prevent inadvertent alteration of the lamps' beam.

The hand-brake lever is set between the tunnel and the driver's left leg, which is not at all a bad place for it. It is necessary to reach only slightly for the grip. The lever has a fly-off action, being locked by a button. It holds the car securely.

The remote gear-lever is one of the charms of the TR2. Very conveniently placed, it is truly short and rigid, enabling rapid gear changes to be made. The action is somewhat harsh, but this is largely masked by the short travel of the lever, which is spring-loaded to safeguard selection of reverse. There is useful synchro-mesh, but so readily does the engine respond to the throttle that double-declutching will be the usual method of swopping ratios. Some idea of the step-up of the gearbox is afforded by remembering that 2,000 r.p.m. is equal to a speedometer 10 m.p.h. in first gear, 20 m.p.h. in second gear, 30 m.p.h. in third gear, 40 m.p.h. in top gear and 46 m.p.h. in overdrive top. In normal top gear the needles of speedometer and rev.-counter move upwards in roughly the same plane. The speedometer has about the usual degree of optimism, so that the magic 100 m.p.h. is indicated at an actual speed of about 94 m.p.h.

The clutch is smooth, light and slip-free but the pedal has to be pressed down fully to ensure easy engagement of bottom cog.

That about completes the " cockpit-drill," except to mention that the horn button, in the wheel centre, operates a rather mediocre, blatant horn, that the central rear-view mirror is a trifle shallow and that there are normally no fog or spot-lamps. The flashing-type direction-indicators are self-cancelling, brought into action by an excellent flick-switch on the steering-wheel hub.

On the road the Triumph TR2 gets along as its performance on paper suggests it will—which is certainly not hanging about ! The engine only begins to sound and feel as if it is working at beyond 4,000 r.p.m. and is quite happy up to its maximum, although normally not much above 4,000/4,500 r.p.m. is necessary to obtain full acceleration. Over 50 m.p.h. is obtainable in second speed and nearly 80 in third (indicated speeds).

The TR2 is reasonably hard-sprung, so that it does not wallow when cornering or dip its nose excessively under braking. This gives rise to some up and down motion of a rather lively kind, but generally the ride is exceptionally comfortable, even during negotiation of unmade roads.

The steering is light and smooth at speed, is geared 2⅛ turns lock

SENSIBLE.—This photograph of the TR2's dashboard shows how speedometer and tachometer are set before the driver, the other instruments grouped centrally, the short remote gear lever, position of the hand-brake and the overdrive-button on the extreme right of the dashboard.

to lock, provides a reasonable turning circle and transmits practically no kick-back. There is mild castor action, a minimum of free play at the wheel, and column vibration is evident only when bad surfaces set up scuttle-shake, which becomes considerable under adverse conditions, and is particularly evident to the passenger.

Although the occupants sit rather low, both front lamps and wings can be seen, in spite of the wide bonnet.

The Triumph holds the road very well under conditions known to enthusiasts as 6/10ths.* In cornering there is an oversteer tendency, leading to sudden rear-end breakaway. The steering feels " light " and would probably be improved by increased castor action, and could be rather higher geared for speed work. The rear wheels hold down well when accelerating, wheelspin, however, being easily promoted in the wet on the lower gears. There is a faint suspicion that the rear axle is not quite positively located, but in general the TR2 is a safe, charming motor car in which to travel.

The Lockheed hydraulic brakes are reasonably powerful but fierce under a light pedal depression, whereas more progressive braking would be preferable. Under the conditions of our test they proved vice-free and had the merest trace of a squeal. Tyre squeal, too, was at a minimum.

It is also a useful car from the touring viewpoint, in spite of its sports-car characteristics, for the luggage boot is of sensible capacity. Its broad lid requires a carriage-key to open the two locks, which isn't exactly convenient, and there is no handle by which to raise the lid, but we can forgive this due to the amount of luggage which can be carried, with the spare wheel located in a compartment of its own, beneath and entirely separate.

Powerful rear lamps, three in number, are reasssuring and the headlamps, which, being neither completely built-in nor " old-school," are ugly, give ample light in the full-beam position but require adjustment.

Normally the TR2 will be enjoyed as an open car, when the cut-away sides to the doors and absence of folded hood provide excellent all-round visibility. Erection of the sidescreens renders the car very comfortable even in winter and the hood is likely to be used only in heavy rain or at the request of a member of the fair sex. It is separate from its frame, which is substantial. The material is good, with good-quality press-buttons requiring strong manipulation; once in place there is ample head-room and good visibility, while a large rear window offers useful vision for reversing unless obscured by rain or condensation. We had no opportunity of

* This refers to the Birkett Dicing Analysis, which, expressed briefly, can be quoted as follows :—

1/10th : Elderly Dodderer taking it easy.
2/10ths : Elderly Dodderer going somewhere.
3/10ths : Commercial Traveller concerned main y with Mi'eage between Overhauls.
4/10ths : Most leisurely progression practised by One of Us.
5/10ths : Slowest form of Rally-driving, when right on time.
6/10ths : Everyday motoring when a trifle late or getting time-in-hand on a rally.
7/10ths : No risks taken and could maintain all day, but glad Elderly Dodderer is not on back seat.
8/10ths : Keen type taking Editor of a Motoring Journal for a demonstration run. (This constitutes the main risk in this profession.)
9/10ths : Racing driver doing his desperate best under a " faster " signal from his pit.
10/10ths : Dangerous motor-bandit hotly pursued by entire C.I.D. in Ferraris. Inevitably results in an accident.

PROVING ITSELF.—The Triumph TR2 seen in action, on the left in the Alpine Rally and, on right, at Le Mans where, although outclassed in respect of sheer speed, No. 62 finished intact, with a very modest fuel consumption.

testing the waterproof qualities in torrential rain and a few gaps where such rain might penetrate were noticeable, but under ordinary wet conditions the protection is 100 per cent. Simple yet sensible, the sidescreens fit snugly into metal sockets on the doors, with clamp screws, and press-slots to hold them to the doors.

The interior of the car provides plenty of room and does not become contaminated by fumes or heat. There is space behind the bucket seats for stowage of soft objects, but the curve of the boot-wall and cover over the back axle prevent provision of a flat floor. No tonneau cover came with the test car but one is normally provided. There is an unobtrusive grab-handle for the use of nervous or gymnastic passengers.

Under-bonnet accessibility is good; the top panel is openable after pulling a knob beneath the dash on the off side and releasing a simple safety-catch. The Vanguard engine in sports form is vice-free, not pinking and only running-on after being switched off towards the later part of the test. Oil consumption worked out at 2,800 m.p.g., and fuel consumption, driving hard, at 27/28 m.p.g. It starts easily in cold weather, given sufficient choke; the choke-knob has to be held out by hand, not appearing to lock, although it constitutes also a hand-throttle.

Apart from its very fine performance, the Triumph TR2 is surprisingly economical. The splendid fuel economy of the TR2 was a feature of last year's sports-car races and owners can congratulate themselves on this very useful aspect of this highly-attractive car.

In conclusion, the Triumph TR2 may not possess "character" to any appreciable degree, but as a vice-free sports car of modest price and fuel-thirst, no one with £887 to spend can afford to ignore it. It is a desirable addition to the British market and that such a car can be successfully constructed from standard components is a tribute to the more sober cars for which such components were intended.

The Triumph Motor Company, moreover, will obviously develop

its excellent TR2 still further, and as it operates a TR2 Owners' Club, with mods.-log-book, badge and promulgation of competition success by amateur drivers and offers a useful list of optional extras for improved comfort and performance, this already firmly-established sports model clearly has a rosy future ahead of it.—W. B.

THE 2-LITRE TRIUMPH TR2 TWO-SEATER

Engine : Four cylinders, 83 by 92 mm. (1,991 c.c.). Push-rod o.h.v. 8.5 to 1 compression ratio. 90 b.h.p. at 4,800 r.p.m.

Gear ratios : First, 12.5 to 1; second, 7.4 to 1; third, 4.9 to 1; top, 3.7 to 1; overdrive, 3.03 to 1.

Tyres : 5.50-15 Dunlops on centre-lock wire wheels.

Weight : 18 cwt. 2 qtr., without occupants, but ready for the road with approximately one gallon of fuel.

Steering ratio : $2\frac{1}{3}$ turns, lock to lock.

Fuel capacity : $12\frac{1}{2}$ gallons.

Wheelbase : 7 ft. 4 in.

Track : Front, 3 ft. 9 in.; rear, 3 ft. $9\frac{1}{2}$ in.

Dimensions : 12 ft. 7 in. by 4 ft. $7\frac{1}{2}$ in. by 4 ft. 2 in. (high).

Price : £625 (£886 10s. 10d. with p.t.).

Makers : The Triumph Motor Company, Ltd., Coventry.

N.B.—On the car tested the heater, overdrive and wire wheels were extras. Other extras include cast-alloy sump, stiffer front springs, larger back shock-absorbers, aero-screens, undershield, rear spats, leather upholstery, metal cockpit cover, radio, tool-roll with tools, telescopic steering column, Road Speed tyres, two-speed screen-wipers, fitted suitcase, and dished steering wheel. The test car was red; white, green or black also available.

AUTOSPORT, SEPTEMBER 27, 1957

CLEAN UNDERSIDE and good ground clearance of the latest TR are seen in this low angle shot. The intake grille is a smart feature of the new car.

are commendably quiet. I had to criticise the original TR2 for a noisy exhaust, but this has been eliminated, which greatly increases the pleasure of handling the car.

In matters of suspension and road-holding, I am raising my sights all the time. Thus, a car which called forth extravagant praise a few years ago might be regarded as being merely adequate today. This is natural as techniques improve, and so I make no excuse for subjecting the TR3 to a very searching test.

I would regard the Triumph as being a very safe car in the hands of the average driver. This is because it does not at first give the impression of holding the road particularly well. With experience, one finds that the adhesion is in fact

JOHN BOLSTER
TESTS THE
TRIUMPH TR3

Disc brakes and over 100 b.h.p. in the latest version of one of the world's most popular sports cars

WHEN I performed the first road test of the then new Triumph TR2, I predicted a great success for it. My prophecy proved to be abundantly true, and this 2-litre sports car became one of the world's most popular speed models. Now, I have revived memories of that very first Triumph by testing its broadly similar successor, the TR3.

The TR3 retains the well-tried box-section frame, which is supported on wishbones and helical springs in front, and passes beneath the hypoid axle, from which it is suspended on underslung semi-elliptic springs. The engine now has larger S.U. carburetters, and is rated at 101 b.h.p. at 5,000 r.p.m. on a compression ratio of 8.5 to 1. It has a cast-iron block with wet liners and a three-bearing crankshaft, while the conventional pushrod-operated valves seat in an iron head.

The four-speed gearbox with remote control was one of the best features of the TR2, and this is unchanged. The optional Laycock-de Normanville overdrive was fitted to the test car. The

disc-type front brakes were an interesting refinement. The two-seater body retains the bluff but not unattractive appearance which we have come to know so well, and is notable for its extremely useful luggage accommodation. Sports cars are often used for long-distance touring, yet they very rarely have adequate room for baggage. The Triumph must be particularly commended in this respect.

The hood, as always, is excellent, and the sidescreens are of a new and more attractive pattern. Entry and exit are not unduly difficult for such a low car. The seats are comfortable and have plenty of adjustment, while all the controls and instruments are well placed.

Hot or cold, the engine starts at once, and the clutch takes up smoothly as one moves off. The gearbox is just as delightful as always, and the indirect ratios

better than it at first appeared, and the machine is always very controllable. Yet, for some reason which is not easy to define, it does not encourage the man at the wheel to take undue risks.

The cornering power is not exceptionally high, but when the limit is reached and the car slides, it remains perfectly easy to handle. The rear end does break away, but quite gently and with no undue tendency to spin. The rear semi-elliptic springs are commendably free from "winding up" during acceleration. The ride is definitely hard, but an acceptable degree of comfort is given on smooth British roads.

Thus, the Triumph forms a perfectly practical method of everyday transport, and with hood and sidescreens erect it would do very well for evening dress occasions. The car is flexible and has good traffic manners, and the lively

COMPACT dimensions and a neat, clean body style are evident. The Triumph manages to look equally elegant and functional—a rare combination—whether the hood is raised or folded away. Useful luggage accommodation is provided and the car is a practical form of everyday transport.

AUTOSPORT, SEPTEMBER 27, 1957

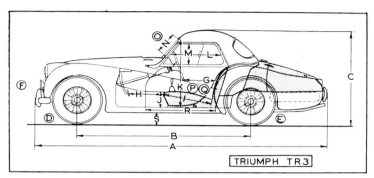

TRIUMPH TR3

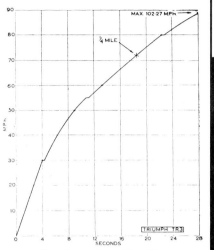

Acceleration Graph

A Overall length, 12 ft. 6½ ins.
B Wheelbase, 7 ft. 4½ ins.
C Overall height, 4 ft. 2½ ins.
D Front track, 3 ft. 10½ ins.
E Rear track, 3 ft. 10 ins.
F Overall width, 4 ft. 8½ ins.
G Squab to steering wheel, 1 ft. 2 ins. min.; 1 ft. 8 in. max.
H Cushion to accelerator pedal, 1 ft. 3 ins. min.; 1 ft. 9 ins. max.
I Depth of seat cushion, 1 ft. 9 ins.
J Height of seat cushion, 8 ins.
K Height to top of screen frame from floor, 3 ft. 0 ins.
L Width of side screen, 2 ft. 1½ ins.
M Depth of side screen, 10½ ins.
N Depth of windscreen, 11½ ins.
O Width of windscreen, 3 ft. 6½ ins.
P Width of seat cushion, 1 ft. 6 ins.
Q Overall width of seats, 3 ft. 9 ins.
R Door width, 2 ft. 1½ ins.
S Ground clearance, 6 ins.

acceleration is a potent safety feature in the right hands.

The powerful 2-litre engine naturally gives a very real performance to this small and relatively light car. A genuine, timed 100 m.p.h. can be exceeded on top gear, and on the overdrive a three-figure speed can also be attained, though the direct drive is a little faster. Third is a really splendid gear, and can be used right up to 80 m.p.h. for overtaking.

Curiously enough, this TR3 was fractionally slower than "my" original TR2. I have come to the conclusion that the earlier car was one of those lucky accidents—an exceptionally good one—whereas the TR3 was a more average sample. Fundamentally, the later model should have more power and therefore speed. In any case, the performance is all that any normal owner could desire.

I have spoken of the improved silencing. Another criticism that I made in my original road test concerned the brakes. The current car has the front discs which are now standard, and these really do overcome the fading troubles. In the past, the rear brakes of Triumphs have not always stood up to their work, but some time ago the drums were increased in size, and all is now well. The man who drives on his brakes is a bad driver, but even he will be unable to overheat the "anchors" of the TR3. This is certainly the biggest single improvement that has been made available on the new car.

From an engineering point of view, this is a soundly constructed machine with nothing flimsy about it, and should stand up to plenty of hard driving. It is a straightforward vehicle for servicing, and provided that one has a pit or hoist, the general accessibility is quite satisfactory. Any owner who carries out the maintenance of an ordinary saloon will find the Triumph just as easy to keep in proper tune.

The TR3 is a fast and economical sports car, and by modern standards it is moderately priced. It has enough performance for competition work, but it is as a fast, long-distance touring car that it excels. Above all, it is a practical machine with good weather protection, adequate creature comforts and considerable luggage accommodation for a sports car.

FRONT WHEEL of the TR3 looks strangely "empty" because of the lack of a brake drum. Part of the disc-type brake is just visible.

Specification and Performance Data

Car Tested: Triumph TR3 sports 2-seater. Price £1,021 7s. including P.T. Extra, wire wheels £37 10s. including P.T.

Engine: Four cylinders 83 mm. x 92 mm. (1,991 c.c.). Pushrod operated overhead valves, 101 b.h.p. at 5,000 r.p.m., 8.5 to 1 compression ratio. Twin S.U. carburetters. Lucas coil and distributor.

Transmission: Borg and Beck 9 ins. single dry-plate clutch with hydraulic operation; 4-speed gearbox with short central remote control lever, plus electrically operated overdrive (optional extra). Ratios, 3.03 (o/d), 3.7, 4.9, 7.4 and 12.5 to 1. Short open Hardy Spicer propeller shaft. Hypoid rear axle.

Chassis: Box-section frame with cruciform, underslung at rear. Independent front suspension by wishbones and helical springs with telescopic dampers. Cam and lever steering, 3-piece track rod. Semi-elliptic rear springs with piston-type dampers. Centre-lock wire wheels (extra), fitted 5.50-15 ins. tyres. Hydraulic brakes, disc-type in front.

Equipment: 12-volt lighting and starting. Speedometer, rev.-counter, ammeter, water temperature, oil pressure and fuel gauges. Flashing direction indicators.

Dimensions: Wheelbase 7 ft. 4½ ins. Track, front 3 ft. 10½ ins., rear 3 ft. 10 ins. Ground clearance 6 ins. Turning circle 32 ft. Weight 18½ cwts.

Performance: Maximum speed 102.27 m.p.h. (direct top). Speeds in gears, overdrive 100 m.p.h., third 80 m.p.h., second 55 m.p.h., first 30 m.p.h. Standing quarter-mile 18.6 secs. Acceleration: 0-30 m.p.h., 4 secs.; 0-50 m.p.h., 8.8 secs.; 0-60 m.p.h., 13.2 secs.; 0-80 m.p.h., 22.4 secs.

Fuel Consumption: Driven hard, 25 m.p.g.

★

COCKPIT layout is neat and handy. Principal instruments are large and easily visible. The overdrive switch is visible on the right of the dashboard, handbrake lever is of the fly-off type.

★

The Triumph T.R.3 Sports

An Improved Triumph TR3

A New Front and Redesigned Seats

A RE-STYLED front, improved interior trim and external door handles (with locks) are the principal innovations which have been made in a new version of the Triumph TR3 Sports 2-seater which is now in production in both open and detachable hard-top forms.

As will be seen from the photographs on this page, the front panel between the wings and forward of the bonnet opening

The completely reshaped front and distinctive grille of the latest model are seen above while, on the left, the tail view shows the separation of the winkers and brake lights and the new external door handles. Production models will have a boot handle as well.

has been completely reshaped to accommodate a wide shallow grille which now embraces the combined side lamps and flashing direction indicators. The grille itself is slightly more forward than before and the faired headlamps protrude less, their lower portions in fact, now being slightly recessed.

In addition, the word "Triumph" now appears in spaced-out chromium-plated letters above the grille in conformity with the modern trend in name plates. The whole effect is both more modern and more attractive.

Stronger Over-riders

A detail of interest is that the upper portions of the bumper over-riders are now given additional support by stays which pass through the grille and are bolted to the inner wing pressings to provide additional strength for the sort of treatment bumpers are liable to receive in some overseas markets.

At the rear, the tail follows the former lines, but the word "Triumph" now appears in chromium-plated letters above the number plate and the lockable boot lid has a handle. The winkers, moreover, have been separated from the brake lights to avoid any possibility of confusion and the number-plate lamp is now plated. A further small difference

The separate bucket seats have more curved backs to provide extra lateral support and the trim generally has been improved. The central instrument panel is now black.

in finish is the use of silver laquered wheels in place of colour.

So far as the interior is concerned, individual separately adjustable seats are retained, but the squabs are more rounded, bucket fashion, to give additional lateral support and the upholstery is deeper than before. Behind the seats, where there is useful accommodation for light luggage, the trim has also been improved to enhance the general appearance of the cockpit. The layout of the facia board is unaltered, but the central panel has a black lustre finish on the latest models.

Another change which will be very welcome is the fitting of external door handles so that it is no longer necessary

to open one of the sliding panels in the rigid-framed Perspex side-screens in order to open the car when the hood and screens are in use. In addition, both doors lock with a key and the finger-grips on the outsides of the sliding Perspex panels have been eliminated to make it difficult to open the panels from outside the car when they are fully closed. Further, the interior lock pull-cords have been moved to an equally convenient, but less-obvious, position in the door pocket recesses. The result is to make the car much more secure against petty pilfering than most open models.

In other respects these new TR3 models conform to the 1958 specification which is already very familiar to readers.

A23

OWNER'S VIEW

To illustrate the fascination and rewards of owning a Classic TR, I interviewed two long-term owners and regular users of the vehicles, both with the same enthusiasm, but each of disparate ages, views and priorities, and from different areas and backgrounds.

Neil Revington is well known to TR Register members, being the leader of the Somerset group of that Club, and a successful competitor in his 1954 TR2. This he uses as a road car when business demands do not dictate the use of a Range Rover for its carrying capacity. A Mancunian by birth, Neil's life really has been changed by TR ownership, for his knowledge and enthusiasm for the cars has led him to set up as a TR parts supplier and restorer covering the West of England. He purchased his red TR2 in 1970 whilst he was an Aircraft Engineering apprentice living in North-West London, the price paid being £50! He was not looking particularly for a TR at that stage, but merely for something "cheap, fast and eyecatching". Neil describes the car then as "ropey but running". It carried an undeserved MOT certificate, had very stiff steering and was fundamentally unsafe. However, I can confirm from my own experience at a similar time that this specification was common to the average early TR around 1970, when the marque was very much at its low point on the value/care cycle. Poverty being the order of the day, Neil used the car in this state for his everyday

transport, and he counts himself somewhat lucky to have survived the experience. Fortunately, however, he grew to appreciate the car's basic virtues despite the shortcomings of his £50 example. He decided to embark on what in those early days passed for a "full rebuild". This was largely carried out in the open as he had no garage, the work taking place in the car park of the Apprentices' Hostel, where he then lived, in his bedroom and in a borrowed shed! Neil is nothing if not tenacious, and he considers he must have been one of the first of the "body off the chassis" pioneers. The car was put into smart, safe condition and has continued in this state to the present day, gradually being refined and modified into a vehicle fully capable both of dealing with modern traffic conditions and of providing fun and success in competitive events at the weekends without too much in the way of expense. Neil confirms that modern tyres make a vast contribution to road holding, along with uprated springs and dampers and wider than standard wheels. As regards the engine, he uses 87mm Powermax pistons with a stage-three head, and a modified road camshaft, the reciprocating parts being lightened and balanced. An electric fan is fitted, and in this state of tune the engine produces a useful power output, the resulting machine having little trouble in more than keeping up with large BMWs driven by men in suits. Neil finds it a perfectly practical car and he and his wife now carry their baby son in a carrycot that conveniently fits across the space behind the seats. He confirms that he has derived considerable benefit from being a member of the appropriate TR Club, and conversely has handsomely repaid these benefits by his work done in spreading the TR Gospel. Spare parts availability I need hardly add, represents no problem to Neil in his chosen profession! Upon my asking the

man to sum up succinctly the pleasure he gets from his TR, without hesitation he replied "total enjoyment". As regards advice he would give to a potential owner, Neil recommends "buy one, but expect to have to spend money to make it roadworthy, or otherwise one can have an unsafe car in modern conditions, especially in inexperienced hands. Get or create a good example however, and driving enjoyment with some style will be yours. After all, Joe Soap can drive an XR3 fast, but a TR demands some skill and provides considerable satisfaction".

My second interview subject has a very different TR from Neil Revington's TR2. Geoffrey Goodall, who states enigmatically that he has "turned 70", still drives his 1959 TR3A almost daily, having become something of an institution in this car in the Nottingham area. This TR3A is standard and original in most respects, even to having no overdrive and standard steel wheels. What makes it unusual is that Geoffrey has owned the car for 23 years, and knows every detail of its history during that time, for he has kept a daily log of all expenditure, including petrol, since the day of purchase.

When I asked him what he had paid for the car in 1963 and what its condition was then, he instantly produced the original AA Buyer's Report made on the car at the time of purchase. Of course with the car then less than four years old, it was still undergoing its initial depreciation, and the idea that such vehicles would one day become classic and rise greatly in value was far from the minds of all but most far-sighted. In fact, Geoffrey paid £425, and the car was described as being in good overall condition, the report remarking that the big-ends were somewhat suspect, and that the paint work was showing initial signs of surface rusting and marking. The big-end problem was attended to prior to taking delivery, and the bodywork was soon brought up to standard.

Geoffrey had always fancied owning an open car since the early 1950's, when an acquaintance of his owned one of the just post-War Triumph 2000 Roadsters, but by the time he was able to afford his own sports car, the Roadster had become "too out of date", and a TR was the logical successor. Evidently the sight of a dark blue TR2 one Summer evening in 1958 finally made Geoffrey resolve to become a TR owner, although it was still a further five years before he achieved his ambition.

Although he still attends to routine maintenance and cleaning tasks himself, the TR has been maintained almost throughout his ownership by the staff of one local garage, who have of course come to know the car very well. This continuity has had considerable advantages, the only difficulties being with parts supply during the early 1970's, when the local Triumph Main Agents could no longer assist. Fortunately Cox and Buckles Limited came on the scene around that time, and Geoffrey has always dealt with them, finding them almost always able to supply, by return of post if necessary. The car has now covered 143,000 miles and is still taxed throughout the year and in use on most days unless it is raining. A schoolmaster by profession, Geoffrey used the car for his daily commuting up until his retirement in 1975, and even now frequently encounters former pupils, whose invariable first question is "have you still got your TR"? The gearbox is totally original, as is the axle and propshaft, although the original engine was replaced at 89,000 miles in 1970, after developing piston slap and main bearing noise. It would probably have carried on for another few thousand miles, but a 2.2 litre replacement was desired, which was duly fitted after supply on

exchange from the Standard-Triumph works, at a total cost including fitting of £103! Unfortunately, when only 4,900 miles old, this new engine, suffered from the not-unknown problem of crankshaft breakage, the only major malady to afflict the car in the 23 years of ownership. After some letter writing, Geoffrey managed to persuade the Works to re-imburse most of the cost of repair with a new crankshaft, and the repaired engine has been excellent ever since. Incidentally, the breakage occurred at 2,000 rpm when the car was running gently in top gear, and in no way under any stress. Those TR men unfortunate enough to have suffered broken crankshafts have confirmed that it usually seems to happen at low speed, the converse of what one might expect. I do not however wish to overstress this problem, for in general the engine is one of the most reliable and long-lived petrol engines ever built. I have myself covered 100,000 miles in TRs, and have never experienced any crankshaft difficulty.

Bodily, the TR3A has been properly maintained, but never rebuilt as such. Rust, when it has appeared, has been properly dealt with by cutting out and replacement, and while the outer sills and three of the four wings have been renewed, the doors, boot lid, front and rear aprons, and all other body panels are original. The car has never been fully repainted, although it has had a lower half respray more than once. The chrome work, trim and interior are virtually entirely original, and in remarkable condition after nearly 150,000 miles. The original sliding "dzus" type sidescreens have just been replaced and the car has had one new hood. Tyre life on Michelin "XAS" Radials has been excellent, 50,000 plus miles per set. The only extras fitted are a Standard-Triumph anti-roll bar and aluminium sump, Koni front shock absorbers, a reversing

lamp and a period-type map light. The car appears remarkably well preserved and is a credit both to its owner and the garage that looks after it. It has never been entered for any form of competition, neither of the driving nor of the polishing type, as such events have no appeal for the owner. When early in 1970 the formation of a TR Club was proposed by Terry Simpson, Geoffrey sent his application in immediately, becoming member number 33 of the TR Register, to which he has belonged ever since. Although not a regular meeting attender, he has continuously maintained his membership, finding the Club Magazine an excellent way of keeping in touch with other owners and with developments relating to spares supply.

Upon being asked for his advice to any prospective TR buyer, Mr. Goodall's words were "buy one, and hold on to it – driving the car is a rejuvenation tonic". Taking his TR out knocks 20 years off his age is his claim, and he still really enjoys the sensation of driving a machine that is fast enough to provide a thrill, and turns heads into the bargain!

Both owners agree that the TR performance is excellent, especially having regard to the car's age, and that running costs are moderate, even when garage maintained, provided one knows one's garage and stays with it! They can both give the model unqualified recommendation, and as long-term owners, such recommendation must be of value. The only caveat is that even a fully rebuilt car will need care and attention to keep it safe, roadworthy and looking smart; 30-year-old cars cannot be treated as modern ones with their 12,000 mile service intervals, and provided this is realised, both owners feel sure that any prospective TR purchaser who takes the plunge will never regret his choice.

British Racing green paintwork, wire wheels and cut-away doors combine to produce a distinctly sporting look. The simple, uncluttered styling of the TR2 is shown here, representing the first generation of one of the World's most successful sports cars

These rear views of the TR2 enhance the impression of ruggedness and fitness for purpose. No frills, no unnecessary embellishment and an overall effect combining style with practicality.

Viewed head-on, the narrow track of the TR is apparent. The "open mouth" represented a very efficient cooling duct, an efficiency lost to some extent with the TR3A's wider grille.

The engine and ancilliaries were easily accessible within the wide engine bay, unless of course work was needed on the radiator!

Leather trim was optional throughout the production run, but was not commonly specified. Red trim as originally supplied was somewhat darker than this retrimmed example.

Signal Red was the commonest exterior colour, and suits the TR particularly well. The cellular grille identifies this car as a TR3.

The standard fitment disc wheels with chromium nave
plates are demonstrated in this side view of the TR3.

Quiet country roads, aeroscreens and a TR3 ready to go
– what more could a keen TR man desire? (a blonde,
perhaps?)

Main picture: *Frontal styling differences between the three models can be compared in this view. Taken overall however, the model remained remarkably unchanged during the production run of almost 10 years.*

Above left: *A three-quarter rear view of a TR3A, hood down but with sidescreens in place. A pleasant way to motor, with freedom from wind buffeting.*

Above centre: *The TR3A shows off its "face-lift" grille. Two-tone colour schemes could be obtained to special order from the works, but were never officially listed.*

Above right: *The TR hood was neat and fitted well. It was much easier to erect single-handed than that of the contemporary MGA or Austin-Healey 100, and adequately weatherproof if in good condition.*

THE TRIUMPH SPORTS

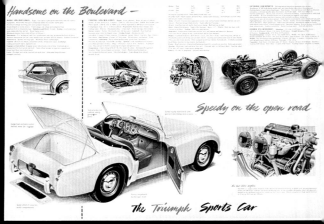

The cover page from the first edition of the TR2 sales brochure, dated July 1953. Note that the car is left-hand drive. Unlike some contemporaries, Triumph used artists' impressions on their brochures, rather than photographs of actual cars. (Courtesy Austin-Rover Group).

An interior page from an early TR2 brochure, featuring the "long-door" model. The "Handsome on the Boulevard" wording and left-hand drive indicates that the sales department had the USA market in mind. (Courtesy Austin-Rover Group).

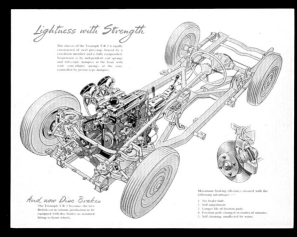

A page from the later TR3 brochure, detailing the 1957 model fitted with disc brakes. (Courtesy Austin-Rover Group).

This brochure cover states "Triumph TR3 Sports", yet the cars are clearly 3As; the Standard-Triumph company continued to use the designation TR3 for the TR3A model for some time after its introduction. The blue car appears somewhat disproportionate, in the manner of 1950's artists' impressions! (Courtesy Austin-Rover Group).

The modified, road-going engine in Neil Revington's TR2. Twin 45DC0E Weber carburettors are fitted, the pipes leading to the air cleaners being part of a water injection system that the owner had been testing. Access to the dynamo must be somewhat restricted by the carburation change!

A nicely-kept TR2 spotted at a recent TR Register National meeting. The car has a Coventry registration mark, sometimes a clue to use when new by the Works for publicity, development or competition purposes. (Photo – Author)

A general view taken at a TR Register gathering some years ago. As a contrast to today's pristine cars, the disreputable blue TR was typical of the condition of many TRs in the early 1970's. Then belonging to the author, this car was purchased in running order for £90! Despite the TR3A grille, TR6 wheels and the presence of door sills, XBD 29 was in fact a very early TR2 in disguise, commission number TS429. (Photo – Author)

Super Profile

Two photographs illustrating the contemporary TR racing scene, showing the highly-developed and successful TR3 of Darryl Uprichard. The car can be seen both in action in a classic car race at the Montlhery track near Paris in 1983, and also at rest, showing off its negative camber. Despite many modifications, the car is evidently still capable of being driven on the road! (Photographs courtesy of Darryl Uprichard)

BUYING

Broadly speaking, these cars today fall into four categories: firstly, and probably the most unusual, is the genuine, original, fully maintained-from-new TR, with a known history. Such cars do exist, but very rarely come on to the open market. They are mostly known to the TR Clubs, and when one does become available, it would normally be sold by word of mouth. The chances of finding such a car are very slim, and for the purposes of this exercise should probably be discounted. Secondly, one has the "fully restored" car. Unlike the first category, these can be created today, and their numbers are in fact gradually increasing as more people either finish rebuilds, or find it worthwhile to employ specialists to renovate their cars. The quality of restored TRs can vary enormously, and this is the area of TR buying where the unwary can most get caught financially. Thirdly we find the "good everyday cars", the true, working TRs. These cars, or rather the numbers of them on the market, have diminished in recent years; presumably this is because they tend to be owned long-term by the die-hard TR enthusiast, who will do his own maintenance, drive the car regularly if not daily,

be a stalwart of the local Club, and who would rather give up almost anything else than his TR.

When such vehicles do appear for sale, they can often be excellent buys for someone prepared to get his hands dirty, for they tend to fetch only one third to one half of the cost of the fully-restored car, yet are in working order and capable of being immediately used and enjoyed. Purchasing a TR within this category cannot however be recommended for the perfectionist, who will find it as expensive to bring the car up to his standards as would be a much cheaper, derelict car. Similarly, those without mechanical aptitude and faced with having to pay others to maintain their TR would find a car in this category relatively expensive to run, and would probably be better advised to purchase a properly restored car, which despite its higher initial price would prove cheaper in the long run for their particular circumstances. The final category is the "non runner". This type of TR can of course vary tremendously, from the car that is complete, sound, tidy and potentially operational, but for some reason has not been on the road for some time, to the totally derelict, dismantled "basket case" which is almost certainly incomplete, and may have been standing outside for many years. Such derelicts are not difficult to find, and are available cheaply, but never underestimate the time, money and tenacity necessary to make a roadworthy car, let alone a concours winner, from such a set of ruins.

Having regard to the foregoing, the prospective TR buyer must consider his personal priorities; what does he want his car for? As a long term project to keep him occupied on cold winter evenings? As a fun car to take to the pub on sunny Sunday lunchtimes? As a competition car, or as a car in which to attend Club

meetings, and to drive on a regular basis. Maybe he simply fancies the idea of owning a classic sports car, without seeing its drawbacks and limitations, especially in modern traffic conditions. A good, well driven, TR will still more than keep up with the modern hatchback brigade, and probably at less cost, but a realist will know that to drive one can be a thoroughly miserable experience on a winter Friday evening on a wet motorway! Conversely there is no more pleasant way of proceeding early on a bright summer morning. Having established his individual aim in owning a classic TR, and having regard not only to the available cash, but also what is actually on the market at a given time, the enthusiast must decide which individual model would suit him best. There is a school of thought to which I subscribe that states that any sidescreen TR is much like any other, at least from the driving seat. Certainly from that viewpoint it is very difficult to tell whether one is in an early TR2 or a late 3A. Body differences between the three models are really no more than cosmetic, some owners preferring the purity and simplicity of the original TR2 open-mouth type front, others admiring the 3A style grin.

The only important differences are mechanical in nature, and of these really the front disc-braking system of the post-October 1956 cars is the most significant. There is no doubt that this type of brake is superior on several counts, and in addition it comes with the stronger Girling braked type rear axle, well worth having in order to avoid the earlier axle's weaknesses. As regards the moderate increase in engine power from the 90 bhp TR2, through the 95 bhp early TR3s to the 100 bhp later cars, having driven all three types on many occasions I am bound to say that I can never detect any difference in the performance of unmodified cars, only in their fuel consumption. There is no doubt that the earlier cars with $1^1/2''$ carburettors were more economical although this is of less importance now than previously, given that most TRs are kept for pleasure and/or as second cars. What does make a difference however is the extra 150 or 200cc provided by having either an 86 or 87mm bore engine. The 86mm bore was offered as an option on the later 3As, but updating by enthusiasts has ensured that these larger capacity units can be found in TR2s and 3s as well. The torque increase is quite noticeable, and fuel consumption appears largely unaffected. The only difficulty is that it is impossible to tell visually which size engine is fitted without removing the cylinder head.

Turning next to optional fitments available, a great amount of additional equipment was made for the TR, and the potential buyer should take such extra items as are fitted into account when assessing a purchase. Surprisingly, prices asked do not always reflect the value, both in terms of cost and usefulness, of such extras; overdrive has to be the single most worthwhile item, and I would guess that this has been fitted by now to the majority of the surviving roadworthy TRs. Wire wheels are a more difficult subject. It cannot be denied that they look excellent when clean, and do assist with brake cooling, as well as facilitating quick wheel changes. On the other hand they demand maintenance, can look awful when rusty or dirty, are heavier and are prone to "clonk" on their splines when the hub adaptors are worn, which is an expensive fault to rectify. 48 spoke wires were the original fitment, but nowadays many TRs sport the 60 spoke type, which definitely has more margin of strength and safety. The TR6 72 spoke type also fit, but these tend to look somewhat fussy on the earlier TRs. Hardtops, both steel and

fibreglass, are available, but most owners prefer to hang them in the garage rather than fit them to the cars! They increase the noise level in a TR considerably, and really offer no more in the way of visibility or weather protection than does a good hood. Their main advantage is that they stiffen up the structure of the car somewhat, by providing a bracing between the windscreen and the rear bulkhead. In many ways what extra equipment is fitted to a particular car should be as important a factor in influencing a purchase decision as which individual model of TR the car happens to be. Having once decided to purchase a TR2/3/3A, the three models are fundamentally so similar that my advice would be to go for the best condition car one can afford, disregarding type, unless of course one has a very particular personal preference. The difference on the road is marginal, and mechanical updating can and has been frequently performed, although the concours or originality enthusiasts may disagree with this practice. Above all TRs were built to be driven, and pampering comes a poor second.

To turn to the structure of the car, the main virtues are durability, simplicity and strength. The chassis, whilst not totally rigid, is very durable, more so than the TR4/5/6 chassis, despite the latters' relative youth. The tubular outriggers supporting the body near the inner sills can rust through, but replacements are available, as are replacement rear cross-member tubes. The main longitudinal members rarely rust, except near the rear axle where there is a slight upturn. The front cross-member and the central bracing are invariably good, owing to the preservative effects of oil film from the engine. One should always inspect for accident damage, particularly at the front around the suspension towers, for misalignment here can be both

very difficult to rectify and seriously affect handling. There is a bolted cross-tube between the front suspension towers which is sometimes missing, causing flexing. The design of the front suspension is straightforward, although it contains a myriad of parts when fully stripped down. The weak point is the bronze trunnion forming the bottom swivelling medium on each side; these have an internal threaded socket into which the vertical link carrying the stub-axle fits. The idea is presumably that the bronze socket is the wearing part, leaving the vertical link thread intact, which is just as well as vertical links are virtually unobtainable. These are also vulnerable to bending by the car having hit a kerb or similar at some time. New replacement bottom trunnions are easily found, wear in this item being a frequent MoT failure point. Lack of greasing the trunnions can lead to extremely stiff steering, and even to seizure. TR steering is probably the weakest mechanical part of the whole car, being by nature heavy and somewhat vague even when well maintained. On a worn vehicle, the steering can be quite horrible, but with proper maintenance and adjustment, the mechanism can be brought up to acceptable standards – it will never equal a rack and pinion system for lightness and precision, however. Nothing could be less sophisticated than the rear suspension, comprising merely an axle, lever-arm dampers and two "cart" springs. This set up with the underslung chassis gives rise to the car's limited axle movement and consequent reputation for hairy handling. Modern radial tyres have done wonders for early TR road holding, as I can vouch personally having recently driven a car still on old 5-90-15 crossply tyres! The limited axle movement still applies today of course, but with modern tyres and provided the springs, dampers and shackle bushes are sound, the rear end is acceptable and has the great virtues of simplicity and strength. One should note however that the TR2 and early TR3 axles are somewhat dubious, frequently breaking half shafts. They also suffer from constant oil seepage around the hubs which appears insoluble, save by fitting the later axle complete, which is a very common modification. The only other rear end problem encountered is occasional fracture of damper brackets. The crown-wheel, pinion and differential gears almost never give trouble incidentally, and the brakes are well up to their task especially the handbrake. The Lockheed twin-bore master cylinders are unobtainable and must be carefully preserved, but fortunately rebuilding kits are still available, and new hydraulic wheel cylinders are no problem for any model.

When appraising a TR for possible purchase, the engine and gearbox are really the least of one's worries. Many an old TR has changed hands for the proverbial £100 in the past full of rust, unroadworthy, and worn in every department except that that lusty four-pot tractor engine would still pull it to 100 miles per hour! Because of this, the cars acquired something of a dangerous reputation in the 60's and early 70's and were frequently overdriven by inexperienced or wild young men, sometimes with unhappy results. Hopefully this state of affairs is now behind us, with those TRs in use being properly maintained. Given the care that the designers and manufacturers intended, there is nothing unsafe about a sidescreen TR. Indeed they can be enormous fun and must still rank as one of the greatest sports and classic car buys on a £ for performance/enjoyment basis. The engine is good for 100,000 plus miles with regular maintenance, and gearboxes can last even longer unless seriously abused.

The valve gear is often noisy, but tappet noise is a design trait, and usually not important. The only major problem seems to be occasional crankshaft breakage, which can occur without warning and frequently at low revolutions. Even then, the inherent toughness of the design ensures that the car remains driveable, albeit slowly! Being of wet-liner design, an engine rebore is a straightforward matter (providing you can get the old liners out!), as is the uprating of the capacity by installing larger liner/piston sets. The Laycock overdrive unit is also very long-lived given the correct grade of oil and regular filter clearance. Malfunction is usually the product of low oil level, clogged oilways, or ancillary electrical problems. The clutch is more than adequate for the job, but if left unused for some time is prone to stick on its splines, necessitating the "short, sharp shock" treatment.

If the engine is of least concern, the condition of the car's bodywork should certainly be the greatest. Being of all steel construction with several built-in watertraps, dubious drainage and no worthwhile initial rust protection, most TR2/3/3A bodies were looking decidedly sad by the mid-1960's, let alone the mid-1980's. Very few cars in good condition today have not had one full body rebuild, and many have had two, and that's not counting accident damage! Almost all the panels rust, the exceptions being bonnet and bulkheads, and to a lesser extent the front apron panel and doors, and even these go ragged at the bottom edges. Fortunately, replacement outer panels are readily obtainable today, as a contrast to 10 or 15 years ago when they were almost extinct. Not only are they available, but they are reasonably priced compared with other classic car panels, and what is more, the wings and front panel bolt on for ease of rebuild. The entire

bodywork of a car being inspected should be considered suspect until proven otherwise, especially so the inner panels which are both more difficult to repair and more difficult to obtain. Floors and inner sills rust badly, and bodged repairs here are common. Boot lids also rust, and this is one panel where replacements can be very difficult to locate. 'A' posts can break away at the base, leading to floating door hinges and hence floating doors! The quarter panels forward of the rear wings rust badly and are not easy to repair properly, and the rear apron panel, spare wheel pan and boot floor are also very prone to attack. Rear body to chassis mountings sometimes come adrift, leading to disconcerting crashes from the back when negotiating bumps, and although not strictly bodywork, the petrol tank often leaks along its bottom seam, where it sits on a bed of (frequently damp) felt.

Bodywork condition is paramount in judging what to pay for a TR2/3/3A, and if contemplating spending large sums on a reputedly fully rebuilt car, be sure to check that the body was genuinely and thoroughly restored. Ask to see receipts, and check with the rebuilder personally if the car was not rebuilt by the vendor. Part with huge bags of gold only when convinced. The TR is relatively cheap to restore thoroughly, but it is still easy to spend considerably more than its ultimate market value on a thorough rebuild.

Trimming a TR can be an expensive operation, especially as this is not a job most home restorers care to tackle. The vital point here is the presence or otherwise of the correct seats. If missing, it is most difficult to obtain a pair of original seats even in bad condition, and these items have not been remanufactured to my knowledge. Glove box interiors are usually missing, but can be purchased, and the trim taken as a whole is quite durable and usually reasonably intact, albeit scruffy. New carpets can be bought, but steering wheels and horn-push bosses cannot, and are both rare and expensive secondhand. Dashboards and instruments usually survive well, but switch gear is frequently incorrect, and the number of TRs still with their original gear lever knob is very limited! It is these small items, so time consuming to find, that are easily overlooked in the initial enthusiasm to buy a ''bargain''. The danger of there being items missing is greatly compounded of course when acquiring a dismantled car or an abandoned rebuild. Such a car can be a good buy, but do not pay any more than the spare parts value. Rewiring a TR is a straightforward operation for the logically minded, and reproduction wiring looms are available covered either in plastic or at greater cost in the original fabric material. Almost all the Lucas electrical items are either available new from autojumbles or special suppliers, or else can be rebuilt. In my experience they are generally very reliable, although

the earlier type ''long'' starter motors can be troublesome and difficult to find spares for.

In general therefore it can be seen that rebuilding and running a TR2/3/3A is a perfectly feasible operation today, more than thirty years after the last TR2 was built. Indeed it is probably easier now than at any time since the late 1960's from the parts supply point of view, if not as regards cost and legislation, for providing the cash is available, a car can be rebuilt to better than new condition. If contemplating a full rebuild, the ideal subject vehicle would be a derelict but complete car purchased as cheaply as possible. It would be a waste of money to pay extra for a running car only to dismantle and rebuild it completely in any event. One golden rule to assist a novice contemplating a TR purchase must be to take with you someone who really knows and understands the model – an ounce of practice being worth the proverbial ton of theory.

Probably the best place to

find a car for sale today would be via the advertisements in the various Club magazines and journals, for not many TR2/3/3As appear these days in that former TR buyers ''bible'', the Exchange and Mart, although this is still worth a look. The new breed of regional advertisement magazines which carry photographs of the cars for sale can also sometimes produce the odd TR, but the better-condition cars tend to be advertised in the classified sections of the monthly classic car magazines. These also carry advertisements from the specialist dealers, some of whom can be helpful, although inevitably their cars will be dearer than privately advertised examples.

Do not be discouraged, for with luck and determination a suitable TR will be found, and the resulting enjoyment will be well worth the effort.

CLUBS, SPECIALISTS & BOOKS

As would be expected having regard to the vast number of TRs both sold and still cherished world-wide, there is a considerable and increasing number of Clubs devoted to the cars. These organisations assist owners in many ways, by providing and locating spare parts, by collecting and disseminating knowledge, both practical and historical, by providing a united front to deal with any bureaucratic threats and intrusions, and above all by simply bringing together like-minded individuals and their cars for mutual benefit.

Countless worthwhile and lasting friendships have been forged as a result of a common ownership of similar cars, and it is probably true to say that without the support of the appropriate owners' clubs, vintage and classic cars as usable and enjoyable machines would scarcely exist today, such examples as survived being confined to museums, barns and junkyards. Thus to join the appropriate club is, or should be, almost the first action of an owner upon acquiring a car. Indeed, ownership is not necessarily a prerequisite, as many clubs admit non-owners as associates, and this can often be the best way of finding a car to purchase, either through club contacts or via the classified advertisements in the club magazine.

Most large clubs are organised on a regional basis, usually with a National Committee or other central management. The principal British TR Club, the TR Register, is run in this way, and has successfully looked after the interests of TR owners since early in 1970. The National Committee is elected annually, and controls a full time computerised office, with membership and secretarial staff. There are around 40 local/regional TR Register groups, many with their own individual committee organisations. Local meetings are also held all over the UK on a regular monthly or bi-monthly basis. Two national meetings are held annually, the principal event being the Summer International TR Weekend, which attracted some 500 TRs in 1985. Eight national magazines are produced annually, and in addition most local groups produce their own newsletters. The Register has approximately 5000 current members worldwide, owing all varieties of TR. The other British club devoted solely to TRs is the smaller TR Drivers Club, which was formed around 1980. Like the TR Register, the TR Drivers Club caters for all models of TR. It is organised on a regional basis with a central management and it produces a monthly magazine.

In the USA there are a considerable number of organisations catering for the TR models, either specifically or along with other Triumph models, and details of the Vintage Triumph Register and the Triumph Register of America, the two "umbrella" organisations are found in the following address list. As can be seen, there are TR Clubs in around 20 countries and the list grows regularly. Inevitably, it is not possible to guarantee that the list and the contact addresses given are totally correct, as this type of information can go out of date almost before it is assembled, but it is as accurate as possible at the date of compilation.

Britain
Mrs. Valerie Simpson,
Membership Secretary,
The TR Register
271 High Street,
Berkhamsted, Herts. HP4 1AA
Telephone 04427-5906 (business hours) (40 local groups, details from the Club office.)

The Membership Secretary,
TR Drivers Club,
39 Brook Street,
Benson,
Oxfordshire.

Australia
TRs Australia –
R. Potbury,
70 Tallawong Avenue,
Blacktown 2148, or
K. McKimmie,
52 Boronia Street,
Innaloo 6018,
Perth

Also Triumph Sports Owners Association Australia, branches in South Australia, Western Australia, Victoria, New South Wales and Queensland.

Austria
English Sports Car Club Austria –
F. Gnapp,
A-1190 Vienna,
Schegargasse 13-15/13/13

Belgium
TR Register Belgium –
Francis Van Hoof,
Van Aertselaerstraat 2A,
B-2060 Merksem,
Belgium.

Canada
Toronto Triumph Club –
K and J Rickatson,
214 Berkeley Street,
Toronto,
Canada M5A 2X4

Denmark
TR Club Denmark –
Ole Norretranders,
Malov Byvej 294,
DK 2760 Maldv,
Denmark.

France
TR Club France –
T. Robinson,
8 Rue A. Rubaud,
94230 Cachan,
France.

Germany
TR Register Deutschland –
Rolf Molder,
Sallstrasse 61,
3000 Hanover 1,
W. Germany.
and TR Sudwestdeutschland I.G. –
M. Diehl,
1M Klingenfeld 67,
6000 Frankfurt 50,
W. Germany.

Holland
TR Club Holland –
Willem van de Mast,
Hanenburglaan 76,
2565 GW Den Haag,
Holland.

Hong Kong
TR Register Hong Kong –
D. Thomas,
3E Mankei Toi,
Sai Kung,
Hong Kong.

Ireland
TR Register Ireland –
Patrick MacMahon,
7 Bellevue Heights,
Greystones,
Co. Wicklow,
Ireland.

Japan
TR Register Japan –
Susumu Osada,
10-77 Imazudezaike-cho,
Nishinomua City
Hyogo-Pref. 663,
Japan.

New Zealand
TRs New Zealand –

K. Tinkler,
5 Christiensen Place,
Milford,
New Zealand.

Spain
TR Register Espana –
Jacques Parser,
Goya 127,
Madrid 9 Spain.

South Africa
Triumph Sports Car Club of S.A. –
Graham Cheetham,
PO Box 29252,
Maydon Wharf 4057,
South Africa.

Sweden
TR Club Sweden –
Torsten Lundberg,
Sandelsgatan 38,
Stockholm 5-115-33.

United States of America
Triumph Register of America –
President – Joe Richards,
5650 Brook Road,
NW,
Lancaster,
Ohio 43130,
USA.

Vintage Triumph Register of
America –
PO Box 36477,
Grosse Point,
MI,
48236,
USA.

Specialists

By the early 1970's, when the
TR3A had been out of production
for 10 years or so, spares were
becoming very scarce, particularly
body panels. British Leyland

dealerships by then carried
virtually no stock for the 2/3/3A
series, and the many TR parts
suppliers we have today had not
yet materialised. Second hand
parts from breakers were often the
only way to keep a car on the
road, and not surprisingly
sidescreen TRs reached the
"bottom of the market".
Fortunately, with the arrival of the
TR Register in 1970, and the
setting up of that Club's spares
service shortly thereafter, the
situation improved, and has
continued to improve ever since.
The Register's original voluntary
spares secretaries, Pete Buckles
and Pete Cox, found such a
demand for their services that the
Club's spares system was put onto
a full commercial basis with the
formation of Cox and Buckles
Spares Limited. This Company has
expanded tremendously, and can
now supply a vast range of spares
for TR2/3/3As, as well as for later
TRs. They have undertaken
considerable remanufacturing of
obsolete parts to original
specification, and now supply
such parts throughout the World
both as wholesalers and retailers.
The success of this firm has led to
a network of agents being
appointed and growing demand
has caused several other unrelated
firms supplying TR parts to come
into existence, many offering
excellent service. In addition to
parts suppliers, several restoration
and rebuilding firms specialising in
TR2/3/3As have been started in
recent years, some excellent and
some less so. As is usual with
such an individual type of service,
the best way to find a reputable
restorer or supplier is by personal
recommendation, or via the
appropriate owner's clubs. In the
following list, please remember
that inclusion is not necessarily a
recommendation, nor does
exclusion imply criticism.
Inevitably, there are far more
businesses in this field than space
to print details, even were full
details of such firms available.

Restoration, repairs and spares suppliers

Cox and Buckles Spares Limited,
22-28 Manor Road,
Richmond,
Surrey,
TW9 1YB.
Tel. 01-948-6666

Northern TR Centre,
(G. and S. Mansfield),
Sedgefield Industrial Estate,
Sedgefield,
Cleveland TS21 3EE.
Tel. 0740-21447

TR Spares South West,
(J. Neil Revington),
The Garden Cottage,
Grove Hill,
Othery,
Nr. Bridgwater,
Somerset TA7 0JG
Tel. 082-369-437

Peter Cox Sports Cars,
(P. Cox),
89 Fairfax Road,
West Heath,
Birmingham, B31 3SM
Tel. 021-477-7966

Racetorations
(L. Uprichard and R. Talbot),
Unit 3B,
Thornton Street,
Gainsborough,
Lincs.
Tel. 0427-616565

Roadsters,
(R. and G. Soden),
The Old Forge,
Crowmarsh Hill,
Crowmarsh,
Wallingford,
Oxfordshire,
OX10 8EQ.
Tel. 0491-38161

County Sports Cars,
(S. Jenkins),
Unit 1, Old Colliery Yard,
Station Road,
Morton,
Derbyshire DE5 6HN,
Tel. Ripley 874 287.

Classic Car Restoration and Repair,
(P. Marks),
12 London Street,
Whitchurch,
Hants.
Tel. 025-682-3245

TR Enterprises,
(R. Hall),
Haywood Oaks,
Blidworth,
Notts.
Tel. 0623-793807.

TR Improvements,
16 Carnarvon Road,
South Woodford,
London E.18.
Tel. 01-505-3017.

The Roadster Factory,
PO Box 332,
Armagh,
Pennsylvania 15920,
U.S.A.

Moss Motors Limited,
PO Box M.G.,
Goleta,
California 93116,
U.S.A.

Other useful services for TR2/3/3A owners

Flint and Co. Insurance,
(official Brokers for TR Register, with specialist scheme for TRs).
57 St. Mary's Street,
Wallingford,
Oxfordshire,
OX10 0EN.
Tel. 0491-38877

Jim Hawkins (Trimming),
Unit 12,
Thames View Industrial Park,
Station Road,
Abingdon,
Oxfordshire OX14 3UJ.
Tel. 0235-27526

Suppliers of full range of trim and weather equipment for TR2/3/3As.

Triumphtune Limited (T. Hurrell),
Address as Cox and Buckles Limited,
22/28 Manor Road,
Richmond,
Surrey,
TW9 1YB.
Tel. 01-948-6666

Suppliers of competition preparation equipment for TR3/3/2As.

TR Bitz,
High Legh Filling Station,
Warrington Road,
High Legh,
Knutsford, Cheshire.
Tel. Lymm 6830/6841.

Principally suppliers of spares for later TRs, but often able to help with parts for TR2/3/3As, especially where common with later TRs.

Books relating to TR2/3/3As

Except for contemporary magazine articles and road tests, very little material was published concerning these cars for some years. Finally, in late 1972, Graham Robson produced his excellent "Story of Triumph Sports Cars". This book covered all the Triumph Sports models, but included of course a considerable amount of TR detail and history. The book, published by Motor Racing Publications, is unfortunately believed now to be out of print. The next item to appear, which is still available, is the TR Register's "Technicalities" publication, an invaluable digest of practical articles culled from the Clubs' newsletters up to 1976. A second volume is in preparation. Graham Robson, who as a former employee of Standard-Triumph is both extremely knowledgeable and uniquely qualified to write on TR history, provided "The Triumph TRs – a Collector's Guide" in 1977. This again covers all TR Models, and is also published by Motor Racing Publications. In 1983 Oxford Illustrated Press/J.H. Haynes and Co. Ltd. published "TR for Triumph" by Chris Harvey, a comprehensive and well illustrated volume covering all TR models, containing, in particular, a useful section on TR restoration. The Brooklands Books Company have assembled a fascinating and informative collection of Road Test reprints and contemporary

magazine articles in their TR2/3/3A book, produced to their standard format; this is an essential investment for those who take their TR history seriously! In addition, reprints of the official workshop manual and drivers handbooks are available, together with the official Standard Triumph parts list. This latter is a really worthwhile investment for anyone undertaking a major rebuild and in some ways is more useful than the workshop manual.

Unfortunately, as far as I am aware, no one has been able to persuade Ken Richardson to write the story of his involvement with the early TRs in the way that Geoffrey Healey has set down his Austin-Healey memoirs. Now that would be an intriguing volume!

PHOTO GALLERY

1. An official photograph of the first TR at the 1952 Earls Court Motor Show. The front and central sections are largely as eventually produced, but the tail is quite different. The front over-riders and sidelights were unique to this car, and the windscreen differs from the TR2 item. The front wings continued below the bumper, unlike the production TR2. (Courtesy of Austin-Rover Group)

2. This rare photograph taken in Montreal in Autumn 1953 shows TS1, the first production TR2, which was sent to Canada for the 1953 Canadian Motor Show, hence the presence of 1953 Ontario number plates. Note the small single hood backlight, and that the car appears to be fitted with rear wheel spats. The gentleman with the car is C.D.S. Phillips, then the Managing Director of the Standard Motor Co. (Canada) Limited. He used the car as a demonstrator and as personal transport for about a year, including some successful competition use. This car is currently being restored in the U.S.A.

3. Another interesting photograph, believed previously unpublished. Dated 20th September, 1953, prototype TR2 MVC 575 is seen ascending Prescott Hill Climb, although it seems to be touring rather than competing. It is possible to see the unique front badge carried by this car. The driver looks to be Ken Richardson, the car being left-hand drive, of course. (Courtesy of National Motor Museum, Beaulieu)

4. MWK 950 was another prototype TR seen here in a works photograph sporting rear wheel spats and what I would guess to be a prototype hardtop, with wider than standard backlight. The two-coloured sidescreen is of the early non-sliding type. (Courtesy Austin-Rover Group)

5. J.C.S. Heathcote's TR2 competes in a driving test forming part of the 1954 M.C.C. National Rally. The venue is Hastings sea-front and the photograph nicely captures the flavour of 1950's rallying, down to the navigator's duffle-coat! (Courtesy "Motorsport" magazine and L.A.T. Photographic)

6. An excellent shot of 4 TR2s assembled for the Circuit of Ireland Rally in 1954. Presumably taken before the start, as the cars are clean. The personnel are believed to be, left to right, Barry Davies, Peter Reece, Bobby Dickson, Mary Walker, Jack Emmerson, Muriel Dodds, Lyndon Mills and Beryl Mills. (Courtesy Belfast Telegraph Newspapers)

7

8

9

7. A night rally during the TR2's heyday. This car is believed to have belonged to Earl Howe, but I have been unable to confirm this, or to find the source of the photograph. Another TR2 waits behind. A lovely period picture!

8. This gem came to light at the National Motor Museum. Five works TR's in convoy, with the leading car receiving attention. No details are given, but I would guess 1955, somewhere in Northern France or Belgium. The last 2 cars are probably PKV 697 and PKV 698 and the man nearest the camera, himself taking a photograph, would seem to be Ken Richardson. (Courtesy National Motor Museum, Beaulieu)

9. June 25th 1955, and the Eastern Counties Motor Club race meeting at Snetterton, Norfolk, included a 10 lap race purely for TR2s. Spins were the order of the day, as can be seen! (Courtesy "Motorsport" magazine and L.A.T. Photographic).

10. A contemporary advertisement for the 1955 model TR2, hence the door sills. Note that the lady is doing the driving! "IT", as was explained in another advertisement, stood for Internationally Tested – a peculiar sort of Standard-Triumph publicity department pun. (Courtesy Austin-Rover Group)

11. A 1957 advertisement for the then newly announced TR3 with disc brakes. (Courtesy Austin-Rover Group)

12

13

14

15

12 & 13. Two views of the TR3A production line at Canley, Coventry. The cars appear largely complete, some even having nave-plates fitted. Blanking plates fill the headlight holes, and were presumably left in situ for the export journey as these cars appear to be left-hand drive. (Both courtesy of Austin-Rover Group)

14. A TR3A competes in the 1959 Monte Carlo Rally, and is seen near the finish. This would seem to be a private rather than a works entry. Note the extra jacking point beneath the door sill, and the item on the bonnet – a primitive spoiler, or a fly deflector? (Courtesy National Motor Museum Beaulieu)

15. One of the 1958 Triumph works team cars. VHP 529 which survives today restored by a British enthusiast. The car was finished in the special "apple green" paintwork of the works team, and sports winter tyres and the roof-mounted swivelling spotlamp, now illegal I believe. (Courtesy Austin-Rover Group)

16. WVC 251 does not appear to have been a works car, although it is numbered consecutively to the 1959 works cars WVC 247 to WVC 250. Probably the property of a keen private owner, it looks to be reposing in the factory somewhere, possibly the competition department. Note the correct, factory-option bootrack. (Courtesy Austin-Rover Group)

17. One of the cars pictured when new in photograph no 8, ex-works PKV 693, surfaced again in the early 1980's driven by Joe Vella at a TR Register Goodwood Sprint meeting. (Courtesy Stephen Wolf)

18. Another ex-works car, this time a TR3 despite the 3A grille. TRW 735 was in the 1957 works team, and has for many years been owned and campaigned by Jon Laver, seen here competing in one of the M.C.C'S classic trials. This car is believed to have covered in excess of half a million miles, and to be one of the highest mileage TRs in existence. (Courtesy S.J. Adams)

16

17

18

19

20

21

22

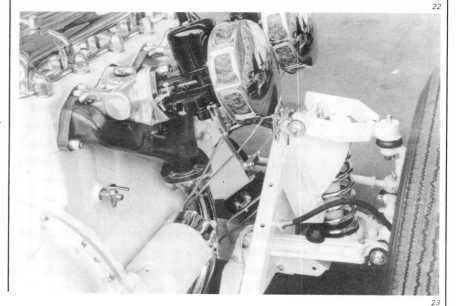

23

19. The modern face of TR racing, which is more popular now than for many years, is shown by this picture of John Welburn in his very rapid TR2 at Lydden Hill circuit in 1985. Reg Woodcock, in his famous white TR, can also be seen. (Courtesy John Welburn Associates Limited)

20. The 1955 TR2 poses when new for the Standard-Triumph publicity department. This model has the door sills below the doors, unlike the 1953/4 cars. Note the painted bonnet and boot hinges. (Courtesy Austin-Rover Group)

21. Another works publicity shot, this time of a new, drum-braked TR3. The hinges are now chromed, and the neat hood-stick cover is in place. Just discernable at the windscreen top are the three hard top mountings. (Courtesy Austin-Rover Group)

22. An early shot of a show-finished TR2 chassis in left-hand drive form, showing the original "double" thermostat housing, and single, short silencer box. (Courtesy Austin-Rover Group)

23. A close-up of the same show chassis, with original style air-filters. These were normally black, the chromed ones here showing some Standard Vanguards in reflection! The domed head-bolts were not standard, and the rebound rubber appears to be missing! (Courtesy Austin-Rover Group)

24

25

26

27

24. The distinctive and clean TR2 "open-mouth" front panel, showing the inset grille and the starting-handle guide. This latter had support bars bolted underneath onto the front tubular cross-member. Later TR2s had a chrome beading around the mouth.

25. The TR3 had a cellular grille fitted in front of the starting-handle guide. Opinions differ as to whether this was an improvement! This car has modern headlights and aeroscreens. The original Triumph aeroscreens are very rare now.

26. The TR3A front differed considerably. The grille, sidelights and bumper were changed, and the headlights recessed. The manufacturer's name was added, but the badge remained the same as on the TR3.

27. The TR3 badge is sometimes plain (as here), and more usually has "Triumph" across the bottom. TR3s had red/black enamel, as did early TR3As. In November 1958, the colours were changed to blue and white, for no reason I have been able to discover.

28. This photograph shows the very rare badge of the Triumph Sports Owners Association, as well as the original TR Register badge. The T.S.O.A. was sponsored by the Standard-Triumph company to assist owners, issuing useful information on the technical development of the TR.

29. This car shows the later (TR3A) rear lighting arrangement, safer today in modern traffic conditions. The centre light is now solely for number illumination, the outer lights are tail lights doubling as braking lights, and separate orange flashing indicators are fitted.

28

29

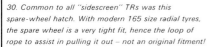

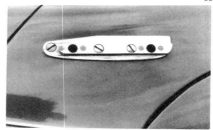

30. Common to all "sidescreen" TRs was this spare-wheel hatch. With modern 165 size radial tyres, the spare wheel is a very tight fit, hence the loop of rope to assist in pulling it out – not an original fitment!

31. This car, although sporting a TR3A type rear panel, is in fact a TR3, hence the "carriage" locks on each side of the boot-lid. (The TR3A had a more civilised handle). The 'T' carriage key is an essential item, for it opened not only the boot, but also the spare wheel door, and the bonnet on all but the early TR2s, which had internal bonnet locks.

32. An original specification, 48-spoke wire wheel, with chromed, knock-off hubcap. These optional extra wheels were not renowned for strength, and have frequantly been replaced by the 60-spoke type.

33. Polished aluminium stoneguards were fitted to the rear wing leading edges, together with an additional section called a "stoneguard foot" in the parts book. Wing beading was stainless on TR3 and 3As, and of rubberised fabric material on TR2s, coloured to match the paintwork.

34. Fuel fillers were these very smart and functional spring-loaded quick-release items. Positioned in the centre of the rear bulkhead panel, they allowed filling from either side of the car, in days when fuel pumps had short hoses.

35. TR2 Windscreen wiper arms were secured to spindles by nuts and cones – no modern, push-on nonsense! Spindle centres on the earliest TR2s were $10^1/_2''$ apart, increased to $14^1/_2''$ later, as shown here.

36. Windscreen mounting plates were fixed to the front scuttle on each side. The screen slid onto these, and was fixed by 2 "Dzus" fasteners on each side, a very rapid operation facilitating screen removal for competition. Later TR3As had bolts rather than the quick-release fasteners.

37. The TR2 facia, with correct switchgear and instrumentation. The rev-counter was red-lined at 5000 rpm, the notoriously optimistic speedometer reading to 120 mph. However, many enthusiasts have had the needle round to "Made in England" when pressed! This car has an incorrect gear lever knob.

38

39

40

41

42

43

38. Earlier sidescreens were fitted with wedges, which dropped into the chrome pockets seen on the doors. The internal (and only) door release on TR2s and TR3s was the trimmed cord shown. The tiny rear "seats" are not original fitments.

39. The TR3A interior reveals the different type of seats fitted to this model, together with the later "Dzus" type sidescreen fixings, which came into use in February 1958.

40. This Standard-Triumph publicity shot shows an entirely original TR3 interior, with the optional rear seat. In this view the front seats are well forward, giving an illusion of legroom at the rear! The rear seat is adequate for children, and an adult can just sit sideways in some discomfort. (Courtesy Austin-Rover Group)

41. A representative TR engine bay: late 1³/₄ HS6 S.U. carburettors are shown here, with non-standard air filters. The chromium rocker cover was introduced during the TR3 production run, earlier cars having a black painted one.

42. The other side of the same engine. The internal bonnet-locks denote an early TR2, and a TR2 type "low-port" head is fitted, but the inlet manifold is for the later, 4-stud 1³/₄" carburettors. Note the brake and clutch combined master cylinder, and the body numbers above the battery.

43. The bulkhead-mounted commission number plate. This style was common to TR2s and 3s, but the TR3A had a smaller, oblong plate, fitted in the same position.

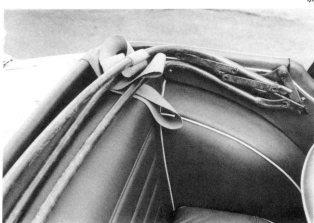

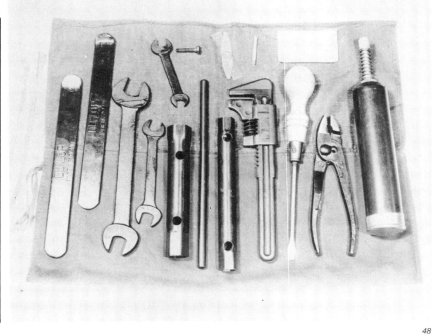

44. A neat tonneau cover was offered as an optional extra. Here shown in half-open form, a pleasant way for the driver alone to travel, retaining a measure of warmth and wind protection. Note the full length "long" doors on this early TR2.

45. Hoods were very similar in all 3 models. The method of fastening differed, however, earlier cars having "Tenax" buttons all round, later cars a combination of "Tenax" and "Lift-a-Dot" fasteners.

46. Hoodsticks folded down as shown, and a neat cover could be obtained, although most owners preferred the full tonneau cover.

47. The TR3A showing the exterior, lockable door handles, standardized with this model. The sliding sidescreens did not have signalling flaps, unlike the earlier items. This hood is fitted with extra fabric covering the rear fasteners, a particularly neat arrangement.

48. The full tool kit, very rarely seen nowadays. I have not been able to ascertain the purpose of the bolt positioned above the tommy-bar. (Courtesy of Austin-Rover Group)